SACRED BALANCE

Blessings in Balance!

Bill D. B[...]

SACRED BALANCE

BILL BLACKMON

SACRED BALANCE
Nobody Wants What Everybody Needs

Bill D. Blackmon
© October 2006

All Rights Reserved. No part of this publication may be reproduced or stored in a retrieval system or transmitted in any form or by any means - electronic, mechanical, photocopy, recording or any other - without the prior permission of the author.

Bill D. Blackmon
1134 Sixth Street East
Saskatoon, Saskatchewan, Canada
S7H 1E3
1-306-343-1605

ISBN: 1-897373-05-8

All Scripture quotations are taken from the New International Version of the Bible (Copyright 1973, 1978, 1984, International Bible Society). Used by permission of Zondervan Bible Publishers.

Published by Word Alive Press,
131 Cordite Road, Winnipeg, Manitoba, Canada R3W 1S1

TABLE OF CONTENTS

Introduction xi

Part I: Everybody Falls

One: Balance: The Overlooked Essential 3
Two: Why *Balance* Is Not a Priority 9
Three: The Perils of Imbalance 15
Four: Places Where We Lose Our Balance and Fall . 23
  *As Individuals 24
  *As Spouses, Partners and Friends 28
  *As Families and Small Groups 30
  *As Small Communities, Clans and Cultures ... 34
Five: Places Where We Fall As Christians
  and Churches 37

Part II: Falling Into Balance

Six: How Do We Know When a Wreck Is
  on the Way? 51
Seven: The Christ Life: A Model of Balance 57
Eight: The Discipline of Balancing 99
Nine: High Road Lonely Road 109
  Endnotes 115

ABOUT THE AUTHOR

Bill Blackmon was born in New Mexico to a U.S. Air Force family and spent most of his early years in Texas with great interests in God, horses, hunting and ranching.

In 1983, the Blackmon family, Bill, Jeanne, Braden and Bowman, immigrated to Canada to serve a church in Saskatoon. Dr. Blackmon has experienced more than thirty years in active ministry. He has acquired Master of Divinity and Doctor of Ministry degrees from Southwestern Seminary in Ft. Worth Texas. He now serves as a pastor to pastors and as a voice for Christian Unity among many churches in Saskatoon. In 1992, Bill became owner and operator of a fishing resort in Northern Saskatchewan. This has been a rich experience combining a love for God's creation, business challenges, and a Christian witness to a lakeside community.

Dedicated to

Jeanne

who has always held me up

INTRODUCTION

As a young cowboy attempting to learn how to ride, an old cowhand, wise in the ways of horses and life, gave me the very best explanation of balance which I have yet to encounter. His words came with a slow Texas drawl:

> It only takes three things to ride anything that walks. You have to keep one leg on one side, one leg on the other side, and your mind in the middle.

I did not at the time realize what excellent advice this was. I thought he was making fun of my feeble attempts. This book, in large measure, is a direct result of attempts to grasp the wisdom of those words.

This book represents an exercise of extreme discipline for me. The subject requires an intensive process of analysis, thought, and rethought. This is not the kind of writing I most enjoy. I far prefer taking all the thoughts and emotions and whirlwinds that happen to blow into my brain and slinging them on a canvas of personal impressions. This *devil-may-care* approach to writing or living or thinking is where the best stuff happens simply because the only thing we usually have to offer to any subject is a unique personal perspective. But the subject of balance will not permit me such freedom.

I have been chided by a number of friends for even pursuing this topic. "Balance is for accountants and fuddie-duddies." "Nothing ever happens when a person tries a *balanced* approach to anything." A popular catch phrase encourages one to "think outside the box". Many consider balance to be the box.

Especially as this subject is related to the Christian experience, balance itself is seen to be a problem. Some Christians are much more comfortable being seen as *unbalanced*. This is a response to the teachings of the Bible encouraging the people of God to avoid conformity to the world. Balance is often defined by these minds as a kind of corrupted conformity. If balance is indeed a box for conformity, it has little value. It is, however, also interesting to note that many of those who belittle and eschew balance have most often left the church a legacy of embarrassment, pain and far greater imbalance.

There is also a sense in which balance is unavoidable. We may find very little agreement on what balance means or how it is played out, but it is hard to imagine anyone who would purposely pursue *imbalance* as a goal.

So let's be honest. Is looking at balance worth your time? This question is best answered by a number of other questions:

- What happens when all the weight in the trailer is only on one side?

- What happens when a kid who weighs 30 pounds gets on a see-saw with a kid who weighs 60 pounds?

- What happens when a plane flies upside down?

- What happens when you place all of your earnings in only one kind of investment?

INTRODUCTION

Are these examples drastically different when they are applied to marriages or partnerships or churches or even large corporations? Probably not. A wreck is on the way.

PART ONE:

EVERYBODY FALLS

1. BALANCE: THE OVERLOOKED ESSENTIAL

Perhaps it is the simplest of all of life's truths: *Everybody falls.* This rule is without exception. Not one single person on the face of the entire earth is exempt. Everybody falls! But that is not all. Every time a person falls, he or she falls for the same reason. It is impossible to fall unless we lose our balance. We are rarely concerned about balance, however, until we fall. *Falling into balance* is the natural human process whereby we learn from our mistakes. Far too much of our falling does not lead us into balance but only sets us up to fall again. Pursuing balance is the only way to avoid falling again. This is true in every area of every life. We always have a choice. We can fall again or we can find the balance.

By nature we move to the extremes. As a general rule, either we are in or we are out. We are for or we are against. We are up or we are down. Talking and thinking about balance goes directly against human nature. We want others to examine **their** thinking. We want to be heard and heeded. We do not move naturally to balance as a conscious process.

Balance becomes, then, the over-looked essential, a critical concern which affects every aspect of every life. Whether we are painting a landscape or a bathroom, building a fence, teaching a math class, seeking to nurture and grow a church, supervising a troop of soldiers or planning our next vacation, if we ignore balance, we will fall.

Unconsciously, balance is as natural as breathing. When our inner ear functions properly, we can walk, run, climb or jump and never give it a thought. We breathe, process food into energy, eliminate waste, rebuild and replace dying cells unconsciously. The brain we are only beginning to understand, has an incredible right side-left side relationship that programs in computer-like fashion the very existence of physical life. Almost all of this amazing work occurs within us without a single thought of its existence. Ordinarily, we think about balance only when imbalance occurs.

If we can recognize balance as an overlooked essential, we will recognize three things: balance is an essential life-component; balance is magnificence in motion; and, balance is not a big deal -- until you fall.

Balance: An Essential Life Component

Balance is essential in every aspect of life. It is essential in physical, mental, emotional, and spiritual health. It is essential in social interaction, economic planning, and political strategy. Balance is indispensable to an understanding of God's word.

By its very nature, anything out of balance is either dead or dangerous. We see the danger of losing our balance while riding a bicycle on a busy street. We may not see the danger of imbalance when it concerns our attitudes and habits.

This is in no way to be construed as a scientific exercise, but the least informed observer can see some obvious truths. Consider the balance which is required for the earth to remain inhabitable. If the force of gravity were to increase or to decrease by only a very small amount, every physical movement of every piece of matter, animate and inanimate, would be drastically affected. If the composition of the air we breathe is altered even slightly, we will be affected. I do not agree with many things which are brought forward by radical ecological groups. One thing I do believe is absolutely true. As inhabitants of Planet Earth, we live in an environment that is totally dependent upon a very fragile balance of atmospheric and ecological forces. And if we lose this balance, we will fall!

Balance: Magnificence in Motion

Balance is synonymous with life. Life exists in balance or not at all. Balance is indispensable, but hard to describe and tougher to define. It is very easy to recognize a lack of balance. It is difficult to explain what makes it happen. All that is physical balance is guided by the laws of physics, gravity and motion. These qualities are but little help in description. With no attempt to wax poetic, balance is beauty in motion punctuated by suspension and empowered by grace. Wherever balance is achieved, beauty is expressed.

One of the greatest qualities of balance is purely aesthetic. Balance has an inherent beauty which exhibits itself in amazing display. The obvious example is the Olympic gymnast or the champions of the circus high-wire. Our minds go to the amazing displays of the swinging trapeze, the spinning plates, or the juggling balls with the master showman gyrating on a unicycle. All are pictures of beauty in balance.

The most beautiful pictures of balance in my mind, however, are replayed in memories of God's creation. I am quite sure that I have watched a whitetail deer jump over a barbed-wire fence at least a thousand times. Maybe five thousand. I am equally sure that I could observe this event a million times and never lose my sense of rapt fascination.

Almost always it is the same. The deer will not jump the fence at all unless it is frightened or there is no way to crawl under it. If there is no way under, the animal will slowly approach the wood or wire, pause briefly, and, in less time than it takes to think about it, sleek hair and supple muscle defy gravity and force, propelling its body upward with the ease of a wind-blown leaf, and the deer settles effortlessly on the other side of this man-made dividing line. Magnificent!

Nothing looks more awkward than an ungainly bird standing in the edge of the water somewhere between Alaska and Mexico. Slow, awkward movements take the Great Blue Heron across the shallow water in search of small fish. As this unimpressive water traveler is startled and alerts to take flight, clumsy awkward turns to amazing grace. In splendor no king can duplicate, the Great Blue arches his plumed head backward and begins a slow melting vaporization before your very eyes. You could not really call it flying. Absent of effort, legs tucked but visible, this ghost-bird transports an unlikely body with an ease nothing short of magic.

Balance: Not a Big Deal Until You Fall

There is no limitation to the number of ways that it is possible to fall out of balance. A few notable examples will give us enough to consider their effect:

1. Consider sleep. What happens when we get our sleep out of balance? Easy. When we have too little sleep we are subject to all kinds of falls. We can fall off our chair, or couch, or tractor seat. Or, we can fall right out of the sky if we happen to be piloting an airplane. Too much sleep can make us irritable and grouchy or prone to depression. Too much sleep can cause us to lose a job or miss the plane to a long-awaited holiday. When sleep is out of balance we fall.

2. Consider eating. When eating is out of balance the effects are very obvious. When we eat too much, we put on weight. When we eat too little, we lose weight. Ditto for eating the wrong kinds of foods. For a select and very fortunate few, eating is never a problem. These lucky individuals never have to worry about weight at all. For the great majority of us, however, we live in a life-long battle with food. Balancing the scales is an issue from which there is no respite. Occasionally, the scales are forgotten for a period of time in complete defiance of this insidious tyranny. Alas, at some point one must return to the torture of the machine on the floor and face the awful truth of reckless disobedience. Back to the diet! Either we balance our eating or we fall.

The issues in our lives which require a constant state of balance are **almost endless**. To a very large degree, the success of any given life is determined by the success with which that individual achieves balance in the givens of his/her world.

Therefore, bringing one's life into balance falls easily under the category of those things which demand immediate and serious consideration. As we continue our thoughts on what we need the most , let us look at some of the reasons why, for most persons, balance is not a priority.

2. WHY BALANCE IS NOT A PRIORITY

The importance of balance is not easy to grasp because we have very little respect or interest in keeping our minds in the middle. There are far more voices in our world crying for extremes than there are voices crying for *balance*. In truth, we do not like *balance*. *Balance* is a pain. *Balance* is an inconvenience. Often in our minds we associate *balance* with mediocrity, lack of conviction and weakness. We are not especially complimented when we are identified as **balanced**. We are complimented to be identified as *radical, extreme, outside the lines*, or *off the chart*. It is hard to interest oneself in a quality for which there is little or no admiration. Why bother?

Nobody Wants What Everybody Needs is not just the title of this book. It is a truth of our world.

These candid thoughts by Wallace Christian truly explain the *balance* battle:

> Sometimes I get so everlastingly weary of being in the middle. Nobody takes the moderate seriously. This is partly because he seldom radiates the emotional intensity of the *true believer* and therefore cannot so easily move the unthinking to dramatic action. It is partly because he is poor copy, and he is a poor candidate for the talk show circuit where guests are chosen to generate maximum heat and minimum light. Can you

imagine "Nightline" with two guests equally willing to see each other's point of view?(1)

Without exception, *balance* is essential to the long term success of every venture. Short term success, in contrast, is often enhanced by a lack of balance. Greater degrees of *imbalance* usually produce the greatest short-term gains. Here lies the real problem.

Examples are in order. Suppose a husband and father chooses to spend ninety-five percent of his available time in pursuit of his business profession, or adding a second job. It is very likely that this person will achieve the goal of additional income. The financial rewards of this pursuit are purchased, however, at the cost of time for his wife and children. If this person's singular goal is maximum income, there is no problem. If his goal also includes the welfare of his family, there are major problems.

In the course of life as we know it, we are often strongly encouraged and sometimes commanded to live *out of balance* in order to achieve short-term goals.

Suppose a fictional financial adviser encourages his clients to sell all their bonds and buy high-tech stocks so they do not miss out on the fantastic opportunities in this incredible world market. The unfortunate persons who did this in the fall of 2000 are deeply despairing today because investing, like every other discipline in life, begs for balance.

It happens in any volunteer organization or church as well as business. There seems to be two kinds of organizationally connected people. There are those who are frightfully over-committed and there are those who do little or nothing. The under-committed feel under surveillance, less than acceptable, slightly guilty, suspicious, cynical, and over-controlled. The over-committed struggle with feelings of injustice, betrayal, and anger because they wind up doing all the work. The over-committed burn out, the under-committed drop out, and neither group finds the balance essential for meaningful belonging.

There are at least five reasons why balance is not a priority of our lives:

- Seeking balance is often a lonely pursuit;

- Seeking balance lacks glamour. It is not nearly as glitzy or exciting as kicking against the fences of establishment or blazing new trails through the unknown;

- Balance demands self assessment and a great deal of difficult thought which many people are unwilling to do;

- Seeking balance almost always involves change. Change is usually forced upon us or ignored completely;

- Seeking balance carries no guarantee that we will not fall again.

An examination of these hindrances can help us assess our own willingness to seek a balanced life.

We avoid balance because it is a lonely pursuit. Invariably there is a large crowd at both ends of any issue or organization and a very small group in the middle. There is always a political right and a political left who are strong and vocal; the voices in the middle are hardly heard. Extremists attract a following. Fundamentalists attract a following. Those who choose to avoid extremist action or the narrow corridors of fundamentalist ideology are usually ignored by the media and criticized by both opposing factions. Admittedly there are those who remain in the middle so they may appear to be neutral or may seek to appease both sides- even this stand is tenuous. Sooner or later there will be pressure from one or both sides to join their cause. The person who stands in the middle as a result of conviction rather than political expediency almost always stands alone.

We avoid balance because seeking balance is not seen as a glamorous pursuit. The crowds become ecstatic, even go berserk, as a result of the actions of the players on the field, but nobody gets excited or even notices the referee until the referee makes a call detrimental to one's team! Then the referee, the man in the middle, becomes the focus of great attention, as well as anger! There is really not much difference in any of life's other pursuits. As a result, a need to be accepted may override one's true conviction. This need for acceptance may create an internal dilemma that is usually tolerated rather than resolved. Inside each person there is the natural desire to be seen as important and capable. This need has the power to move one to the edges away from the center. Even for those committed to the center, there is always the incessant temptation of the edge.

Perhaps it is appropriate at this point to digress, if only briefly, to note that being in the center is not automatically the place of balance. Being in the center can be simply the place of indecision, or, it can be a place chosen to manipulate both extremes.

We avoid balance because seeking balance requires intensive thought as well as serious self-assessment. Thinking is the hardest work of all, which is why very few people do it and those who do it are paid so well. Before one can even begin to think about *balance*, it is essential to understand the forces at work. It is extremely hard work to try to look objectively at anything we really do not like. We as human persons are creatures of likes and dislikes. Our natural tendency is to avoid that with which we disagree. In a true sense we can never be objective about anything. We are positively motivated toward what we like; we are negatively motivated toward what we do not like. It is a great step toward balance when one can identify his/her prejudice. It is an even greater step toward balance when one can admit he/she is motivated by prejudicial preconditions on any and every subject. May God deliver us from those who would seek to present themselves as *unbiased observers,* whether they be educators, scientists, politicians or religious leaders! **Unbiased** observers simply do not exist. **Uncaring** observers exist in droves; **unbiased** observers do not. However, when one who has learned to recognize his/her bias begins to earnestly seek to see another point of view- even if it does not change his/her opinion, a significant step toward balance has been achieved.

It is easy, then, to see why seeking balance is such difficult and demanding work. There are no cheering sidelines, there are many detractors and all too often one discovers the enemy to be one's self.

We avoid balance because seeking balance almost always involves change, not just change for systems or opposing factions-but often personal change. Rarely is personal change achieved apart from pain. It is a cold reality to face the hard truth of human experience. The very last place we look for answers to serious problems is within ourselves. We will explore almost any option before we admit that *we are the problem*. This is understandable basic human nature. No matter how healthy or beneficial it may be, even to ourselves, we will resist change unless that change somehow fits a bigger picture of our greater desires or self-image. In other words, if **you** say to me: "You must change for the sake of balance," I will resist. If **I** say to you: "You should change for the sake of balance," I am only displaying my logical intelligence.

Seeking balance is not a guarantee that we will not fall again and maybe fall harder. The only reason we need balance is to avoid a fall. If falling is not a concern, neither is balance. There are no safety nets for those who attempt the high-wire of balance seeking. Sometimes the search can create even greater imbalance. Individuals are hurt. Leaders are fired. Tempers flare. Friendships are tested or broken. Companies are sold. Churches split. Couples divorce. Nations go to war. Sometimes the best solution may be to live with the imbalance! More often than not, however, avoiding the imbalance multiplies the casualties which will continue until balance is achieved.

What we need most is what we want least. We avoid balance to our peril. To move us toward this courageous approach, we will address the consequences or pitfalls of imbalance.

3. THE PERILS OF IMBALANCE

 This entire chapter can be summarized by one short statement:

Any good, out of balance, becomes an evil.

This statement can be quickly and logically followed with other attending truths:

*Any strength out of balance becomes a weakness.
Any virtue out of balance becomes a vice.
Any belief out of balance becomes dogma.*

Balance is not simply a philosophical or academic exercise reserved for scholars or mystics. Balance is the bread of human justice and the wine of human dignity. When balance is lost, life is cheap and fragile.

Balance is the only truly fertile soil of both social and environmental concern. Almost every existing political, religious or ecological organization represents an extreme. This is true because it usually requires some degree of opposition to create enough interest to acquire enough money for the organization to exist. Wherever balance is lost, human beings and their surrounding environment suffer, and continue to suffer, until balance is regained.

Apart from the pressure of uncomfortable outside forces, we do not normally seek balance at all. In fact, we usually resist it. In order to make a case for balance, it is extremely important that one understand the dangers inherent to an absence of balance. It is almost an insult to repeat it, but too often truth eludes us in its simplicity:

If we lose our balance we are bound to fall.

One of the reasons I enjoy the Bible as I do is the recounting of the very candid people stories which are chronicled in its pages. These are not stories which would have ever been transmitted if the purpose of the writer was to present the players in the best possible light. To the contrary, the people of the Bible are faithfully depicted with all their bumps and bruises, as well as their greatness and glory.

One of the finest of these stories is a family story which could have been written today just as easily as it was centuries ago. The story of Isaac and Rebecca and their two sons, Esau and Jacob, creates not only a timeless family event but also an excellent tool for seeing what happens when life is out of balance. This family picture is recorded in Genesis 25. In fact, the remainder of the book, all the way to chapter 50, is an extenuation of this critical family event. The crux of this powerful event is found in verse 28:

Isaac, who had a taste for wild game, loved Esau, but Rebecca loved Jacob" (Genesis 25:28)

This terse statement carries a weight of great significance. Both parents have a love for a child, but not the same child. Both parents would say that everything they did was for the welfare of all the family. It is doubtful that either Isaac or Rebecca did anything intentionally wrong seeking either revenge or power. As hard as we may try to find him, there really is no bad guy in this story. But there really is a monster in this story, and that monster is a lack of balance in the most basic of human communities, the community of family.

Family balance falls apart when any relationship takes priority over family concerns. In this case we have Mom and Dad favoring different siblings. It is equally destructive when Mom and Dad favor one sibling over another, or when a child becomes more important than a spouse. This is a game which is open to any number of players and it usually lasts a lifetime. What's more, the results are always predictable: everybody loses! There can be no ultimate winners in a contest for family balance.

What makes this story so very intriguing is the opportunity the reader has to see the long term effect of this family imbalance. The plot thickens. To counter Isaac's favoritism for Esau, Rebecca conceives a deception in which she instructs Jacob to disguise himself as his brother in order to receive the blessing of the elder son. Remember that these were twin brothers and that Jacob exited Rebecca's womb holding tightly to his brother's heel. Esau was the elder brother only by a matter of seconds.

> *Once when Jacob was cooking some stew, Esau came in from the open country famished. He said to Jacob. "Quick, let me have some of that red stew. I'm famished (that is also why he was also called Edom- meaning red). Jacob replied, "First sell me your birthright." "Look, I am about to die," Esau said, "What good is the birthright to me?" But Jacob said:" Swear to me first." So he swore an oath to him, selling his birthright to Jacob. Then Jacob gave Esau some bread and lentil stew. He ate and*

drank, then got up and left. So Esau despised his birthright. (Genesis 25:29-34)

The seeds of this contentious imbalance began to unfold long before Isaac's death. It must have seemed very unfair to Jacob to have to play second fiddle to his coarse brother, Esau. After all, he was *elder* by only a very few moments out of his mother's womb. His father doted on Esau's rough and tumble manhood and had little to do with Jacob. Jacob felt disinherited and cheated. Rebecca's concern for Jacob was so great that she entered the struggle seeking to alter the balance of power in the family structure. In an act of blatant deception, Rebecca guided Jacob to a plan that would steal Esau's all-important father blessing and inheritance from him and give it to Jacob.

To put the situation in perspective we also need to recognize the work of the *father of all lies*, Satan, in these circumstances. His extreme subtlety is very apparent. Within this cauldron of family conflict *every member of the family* carries a valid concern, from their own point of view. What is missing is a picture of the family as a whole. Isaac, in obedience to tradition and necessity, was preparing to pass on his responsibilities to the eldest son. That son needed to be strong; he needed to be a good provider, he needed to be capable of dealing with the demands of harsh environment. Isaac was rightly proud of these strengths in his eldest son, Esau. Rebecca loved both of her sons, but her mother wisdom could see that one of her sons was smoldering and dying in the absence of his father's blessing and she moved to alter this situation. Esau, as the blessed son, did what blessed sons do: they carry on their lives, usually very successfully, without a lot of concern for others. Esau did not ask to be the oldest or the strongest or his father's favorite. He just accepted the fact that he was. Jacob sat at home feeling the absence of his father's approval and the plummeting of his own self worth. Therefore, both Esau and Jacob became the victims of an imbalanced family which was created by intentions that were certainly less than evil.

After Jacob successfully deceived his father and brother, Esau vowed to kill him and Jacob was forced to run for his life. He sought refuge with his mother's brother, Laban. Laban, in return, manages to deceive Jacob in a plot regarding his daughters Leah and Rachel. In order to marry Rachel, Jacob agrees to work for seven years. He is tricked into marrying Leah first, and working another seven years for Rachel. Jacob, not to be outdone, plans a deception for his uncle/father-in-law to wind up with ownership of most of Laban's livestock. Having finally *earned* Rachel and Leah and having become the owner of great herds of livestock, Jacob flees from Laban. Laban pursues Jacob and his family. Meanwhile, Rachel has stolen her father's household gods and taken them with her. The picture is at once very humorous and extremely saddening. Lies and deceptions follow one after another: Rachel lies about the gods she has stolen, Jacob collaborates in Rachel's lie and Laban returns home.

Immediately following his potentially deadly encounter with Laban, Jacob, now on his way back home, prepares to meet the wrath of Esau. Jacob is decidedly between a rock and a hard place. It was here, at this point of great difficulty that Jacob encountered the living Jehovah God. Jacob wrestled with God and his life was forever changed. It was here that Jacob received God's blessing and ultimately became the father of the twelve tribes of Israel. Jacob, by the power of God, was able was able to appease Esau's wrath and avoid bloodshed when they met. Therefore, it is tempting to think that the story is completed and everyone lived happily ever after. In truth, however, a generational die was cast that would carry heartache and division for centuries.

Two deadly seeds were carried forward: the seed of favoritism and the seed of deception. Jacob, of all people, should have known better, but he was guilty of the same mistake his father had made in his own life. Jacob had two sons which he favored over the other ten, and that *sin* worked very hard to destroy all of his sons. You can read of the story of Jacob's sons in Genesis 37. Because Jacob loved Joseph more than his brothers, Joseph's brothers devised a plan to *deceive* their father into believing Joseph had been killed by a wild animal when in truth they had sold him into slavery — favoritism followed by deception once again.

The favoritism which was creating hatred among Jacob's sons was fueled by unrest among Jacob's wives, Leah and Rachel. Bilhah, Rachel's maidservant, and Zilpah, Leah's maidservant, were used as pawns. All four of these women bore sons for Jacob. The maidservants entered the picture in an attempt by Rachel and Leah to win Jacob's favor when they themselves were unable to bear children. (Read Genesis 30.) Jacob's favored sons, Joseph and Benjamin, were the children of his favored wife, Rachel. The life story of this family returns again and again to this severe imbalance. This *imbalance* of love, acceptance, and power formed the very foundation of this extended family. A powerful thread of deceit and family rejection continues throughout the history of these families for generations. These brothers became the twelve tribes of Israel, and the pattern repeated itself continually.

Esau's descendants became a branch off of the family tree of the children of Israel. His lineage was not included among the people of Jehovah's choosing. Esau's descendants became the Edomites. Starting in the Exodus and continuing in throughout the Old Testament, the *Edomites* (later *Idumeans*) figure prominently as a primary enemy of God's people. Ironically Antipater was an Idumean, and his son, Herod Antipas or Herod the Great, founded in 37 B.C. the last dynasty of the kings of Palestine who were ruling in the time of Christ's birth. It was he who ordered the murder of male infants in Bethlehem in an effort to exterminate the Messiah.

It all began with a family out of balance.

There are undoubtedly many other descriptive words, in addition to imbalance, which come to mind when one considers individual or family problems. *Dysfunctional* is the most popular word at present for families with problems. Dysfunctional, as a description of family breakdown, is rather misleading because many families with problems are very *functional*. These families often include very capable and talented and wealthy individuals who not only function, but excel. Most dysfunction within families or individuals has as its root some personal traits, morals, ethics, religious beliefs or cultural practices that are admirable and good in their proper context. When these basically good and admirable attributes are elevated or lowered to a specific, and often hard to define level, they become deadly and destructive.

It is so much easier when one confronts an enemy head-on, with a name, a face, a time and a place. It is a tremendous advantage to know who or what is trying to destroy what one values. These are the kinds of enemies that we readily pursue and do all we can to eradicate.

But, when the enemy is our own inability to create a balance of all the good things, not to mention the things that we know are not good, we usually opt out of the problem and look for something or someone else to blame.

A lack of balance is not only the most common problem we face in life, it is also the most difficult to address.

Facing squarely the imbalances which one has created or sustained requires extreme courage and great humility. That is why it is so much easier to find something or someone else to blame, and why many of our heartaches are carried and repeated all our lives. The rewards to one who can recognize and seek to address the perils of imbalance are lifelong and extend to every person who is part of one's world. Just continuing in this book will be an act of courage on your part as you seek the truth for yourself and those you love.

4. PLACES WHERE WE LOSE OUR BALANCE AND FALL

When we lose our balance, we fall. When we do not live up to our own personal expectations or life throws us things we cannot handle, we lose our sense of balance and crash. The evaluations which are placed upon us by other persons can cause considerable discomfort, but not really a fall. No one can create a guilt within us, unless we suspect our own guilt. They may judge us as guilty, and we may have to suffer the penalty of guilt, but until *we* ourselves sense that we have lost our balance, we will do nothing to alter our attitudes or actions. We can be certain, however, that our personal situation will not improve until we can recognize and seek to correct the imbalance that caused the problem. By dealing with a few selected areas of imbalance common to many, it is my hope that we can see, with new eyes, some specific places where balance may be needed.

It is most important to restate the premise of our work. In this exercise we are trying to discover critical areas where we can see for ourselves that we have lost balance or gotten off track. This is not to create or engender the idea of moral relativity. <u>Balance is a not a synonym for situational ethics</u>. Both God's word and common sense dictate that substantive rights and wrongs exist in every area of life. We can be taught to obey without question just by following the rules, but we can never learn balance by following someone else's rules. Even God's rules are subject to a broad range of varying interpretation by a broad range of varied interpreters. One can never leave the hard work of balancing to any other person. There is no one else in all the world who can bring balance to your life. So sit down, take a deep breath, look at your struggle to stay on track, and let's try to learn from our falls.

Places Where We Fall As Individuals

Balancing eating and exercise: It matters not what you may believe regarding personal health and physical fitness. There are many experts who will agree with you, and just as many who will oppose your thought. This subject has taken on religious tones in North America. For many, personal health and fitness is the God which requires the greatest allegiance, the most time, discipline, thought, and money. For some this discipline is not a personal matter but one to be carried with religious fervor to the uninformed masses. It is very difficult in such a society to feel good individually about anything regarding one's health and eating habits because there are so many experts who so radically disagree.

Most experts agree that a balanced diet is essential to good health. Most experts also agree that a balance of diet and exercise is essential to good health. From this point forward- you are on your own. The experts do not agree on what a balanced diet includes or what exercise is most helpful. On this subject we make many, many decisions every day. Our waistline and energy level tell us what kind of balance we are achieving. There has never been more information on physical health and less agreement on how to achieve it.

Finances: balancing what we need with what we want: Just as we search for a balanced diet, we must pursue a reasonable approach to personal money management.

Somewhere in the course of daily living, every person, every couple, and every business must learn the difficult art of balancing what we want with what we need and can afford. This, according to most marriage counselors, is the single greatest contributor to marital difficulty. There are many people who enjoy great success and make large sums of money yet live in dire financial conditions because they are unable to achieve this balance. This balancing act, like what we eat and how we exercise, involves a host of daily and often hourly decisions. Without this balance we suffer great anxiety which affects our overall health and the welfare of every person in our family.

Balancing the use of time: Time, perhaps the most sacred commodity of life, is sabotaged by the imbalance of hurry and procrastination. Between these two destructive extremes there exists a balance of time for every person. Achieving that balance is a life-long struggle. In my previous work, *Faithful for the Season*, a chapter is devoted to the use of time.(2) Almost everyone faces a struggle with time, all the time. In some of life's earlier seasons we struggle desperately with a lack of time. In later seasons of life, many struggle with too much time. In all seasons we struggle with decisions regarding time. Just like food and finance, we are required to make an unending number of decisions regarding time every day. Money and time have much in common. We have a limited supply of both, and we face a series of daily decisions in determining how they are spent. In reality, the very nature of our lives is determined by the way we spend our time and money. When either is out of balance, we are in trouble.

Balancing work and play: It is difficult to admit the need for balance in this area of our lives. Our personal identities are so intertwined in what we do that it is hard to admit that our work or our play is out of balance. We surround ourselves with both the people and the stuff that reinforces our personhood. I am an avid outdoorsman. I have surrounded myself with both the people and the stuff because I love this aspect of my life. Yet, I am increasingly conscious of the need to balance my hobbies with the rest of my life. In contrast, my wife is almost a workaholic. She absolutely loves her work, which is teaching kindergarten children. She is happily and productively engaged in this activity for many hours almost every day of her life. It is very rare, even during holidays, to see Jeanne without some kind of teacher work in her hand. It has been a lifelong struggle for her to find balance in other pursuits.

When we do not balance work and play we experience obvious results:

- too much work-- no time for family or rest or worship or thinking

- too much play-- problems at work, nagging guilt, never satisfied.

- I think we know the routine. What we do not know is how to integrate the two.

Balancing ambition with personal contentment or satisfaction: This is another spin on the work- play dilemma but includes other aspects as well. Without ambition, it is very unlikely we will achieve any degree of advancement. Too much ambition squelches the potential joy in satisfaction or appreciation for what we have.

Balancing social life and private life: Both the introvert and extrovert experience difficulty in balancing time with others and time alone. The only difference is in the quantity of time. This struggle is not an occasional thought. It is a daily concern. The person who tends to be an introvert is never completely at ease when forced into a routine of constant social requirements. The extrovert is equally unfulfilled in a regimen which involves little or no social interaction. For both, a balance which satisfies individual need is essential, although it may be entirely unconscious. Without this balance, most persons find little joy in life.

Balancing caring for others and caring for self: We know the extremes well. We observe some persons who never have a thought for anyone other than themselves. Although tolerated by others, there is no doubt that these people can be trusted only to put their needs above everything else. We also have observed others whose behavior is noble to the extreme, who express no thoughts for themselves and seem to revel in their selflessness and concern for others. It is never possible to judge any other person's motives. However, the very selfish and the very selfless are often on the same page. Both are desperate attempts to find fulfillment and/or acceptance, and both are most often denied meaningful relationship and genuine fulfillment. The struggle for every person is the pursuit of the middle ground. This middle ground is, in truth, the only place where selfish persons find purpose and selfless persons find strength to admit their own, often selfish, agendas.

Places Where We Struggle with Balance as Spouses, Partners and Friends

As we move from the level of strictly personal concerns to encompass the balancing issues common to spouses, partners and friends, it is important to recognize that we carry a lot of *stuff* with us to every expanding relationship. I am amazed to realize the number of places where we encounter a struggle for balance daily, and often hourly, and how the quality of life that we experience, and perceive ourselves to experience, is affected by these encounters. Every day we participate in a struggle for balance. We participate in a struggle for balance as individuals, but that is not all. We bring this individual into every encounter we have every day with any other person or group. This is a powerful recognition and a dynamic which is not to be ignored. Everything that we struggle with as individuals in the balancing act of our lives is translated in some degree to every relationship we experience. It is important for our reflections to carry our personal balance issues to the next level of human contact involving two persons who relate as spouses, partners or friends.

Balancing intimacy with privacy: Daily, as spouses, partners and friends, we struggle for a balance of intimacy and privacy. Our own individual uniqueness legitimately requires these essentials in our lives but, more importantly, this individual uniqueness requires a specific balance of these essentials. Without a balance of intimacy and privacy, the relationship becomes undesirable and even repulsive. This is most true for spouses simply because theirs is the most complex, if not intimate, of all human relationships. Partners and friends, however, who have no overtly sexual or family-demand connections also have very real issues of intimacy and privacy. It is interesting to note, especially among friends, that these issues may never be addressed vocally, but for the relationship to continue satisfactorily, the matter of intimacy and privacy must find its balance or the relationship will soon dissolve.

Our needs in this area are dramatically different. In this and all areas of life, we have a tendency to see other's needs in light of our own. This error is often well intended but disastrous in its effect. The only way a balance of intimacy and privacy can ever be achieved is through the channel of open communication which must include active listening.

Balancing speaking with listening: It should come as no surprise that one of the key elements necessary to developing balance in intimacy/privacy is the issue of balancing speaking and listening. Balance cannot be improved in any area involving more than one person unless communication is achieved. This is a good place to state a cardinal balancing rule: balance can take place in any human relationship only when speaking and listening are accompanied by appropriate action.

It would actually be encouraging if we could discover some new and exciting ways to identify imbalance in our lives. We do not, however, need a lot of new twists to see the problems. In reality, we make the same mistakes over and over again:

You speak, I do not listen.
I listen but you do not speak.
You speak, I speak, neither listens.
You do not speak, I do not speak, no need to listen.

The challenge confronts us every day, and almost daily we fall.

Balancing planning with spontaneity: Once again personality dominates the landscape. Some are prone to plan everything; others are almost entirely spontaneous in their decision-making. Both are strengths, both are weaknesses. Individuals vary in their ability to tolerate the extremes outside their comfort zone, but in almost any close relationship this issue will emerge repeatedly.

Places Where We Fall As Families and Small Groups

The small group, of which families are a natural expression, is the place where societies' values are learned and transmitted. What is known and believed about ourselves, our world, right and wrong, good and evil, love and hate is engendered in this level of human experience. This is true for every child, and to a slightly lesser degree for every adult. The small group/family experience is the garden from which balance and imbalance is grown. With little or perhaps no conscious thought at all, lifelong patterns are encrypted on little brains which are ravenously thirsty for knowledge. The teachers, themselves equally unaware, are transferring their own mix of balance/imbalance to the life equation. Sometimes the transmission is healthy and helpful. Often it is not.

Families and small groups struggle with balance especially in these areas: being versus doing; giving versus receiving; and trust versus mistrust. Keep in mind that families and small groups also struggle with all the previously identified concerns of individuals, spouses, partners, and friends.

Being versus Doing: Whether it is recognized or not, each member of the group has an inherent and indisputable value which is not related to how that person functions within the group. Conversely, every family/small group has very distinct expectations for each person within the group. Herein lies the rub. Because each group is unique, it will support unique values and distinct expressions of those values. In certain families/small groups, acceptance will be the guiding principle of relationship. In such a group, performance will become secondary to acceptance. In other families/small groups, performance will actually determine the degree of acceptance.

Strengths and weaknesses, again, exist in both polarities. The child who feels secure enough within himself /herself without the need to perform may suffer from less anxiety, but may also lack the motivation to accept authority or reasonable discipline. The group member who feels little acceptance and is compelled to constant performance may accomplish much, and yet implode within.

Giving versus Receiving: It almost seems an insult to the reader to enumerate these truths which are so obvious. They are most obvious, however, when we see them active in the lives of others and they are very inconspicuous in our own behavior. It is in the family/small group that we first learn the dynamics of giving and receiving. Birthdays and Christmas, as well as many other occasions provide a regular backdrop for this experience in learning. It becomes apparent very quickly if an imbalance is operating in the giving/receiving arena at these crucial occasions. As children we are more prone to an imbalance in giving, because we naturally desire to receive everything as often as possible. As adults, it is common to see an imbalance in receiving. Many adults, men especially, find it very difficult to receive. Receiving somehow connotes weakness as well as obligation, both of which are to be avoided.

Those who are unable to achieve some acceptable level of balance in giving/receiving are crippled, severely handicapped for life, unless a move toward balance is made. This is fertile ground for almost every psychological problem known to exist. It is a core problem for most addictions. In great irony, a perceived inability to *give* meaningfully to others creates the same powerful poison as the inability to *receive* meaningful offerings from other persons. That poison, regardless of its source, creates a cauldron of intense suffering that is usually generational in its effect and crippling in its result.

Freedom versus Responsibility: Developing and maintaining a balance of freedom and responsibility is a life long concern. This balance is pivotal in the development and well being of every person in every season of life from infancy to mature adulthood. This balance is very important in relationships which are limited to two persons, but it takes its strongest roots in family/small group dynamics. Balancing the infant's *freedom* to express his/her frustrations with the *responsibility* to learn to recognize the needs of others is essential learning with far reaching results. A lack of freedom suppresses the possibility of growth and development wherever it occurs: physically, intellectually, socially, psychologically or spiritually. An absence of responsibility creates selfish persons whose actions create not only annoying, but life- threatening situations. Perhaps it is this imbalance which is most apparently destructive in our world today.

Following a number of generations who focused on personal responsibility, a radical swing to personal freedom has occurred. A large and growing number of very vocal groups grow increasingly insistent in demanding their *rights* with little or no concern for any responsibility. This shift has resulted in a social climate where individual freedoms have become far more important than the welfare of society. Every age group and every race struggles with this issue. Young persons under 21 years of age are often seen as the greatest offenders in this area. However, these *young offenders* have become highly destructive members of society primarily because the law provides very few consequences to their behavior, mirroring the belief in the supremacy of individual expression.

Contrast this scene to the plight of those in certain cultural environments who have little or no choice regarding the matters of their own lives, be it marriage, education, vocation, location, personal property, spiritual or moral values. Without the freedom of choice these persons become little more than slaves, even while being described as *free*.

The need to achieve a balance of freedom and responsibility cannot be overstated. The very fabric of society is dependent upon the creative construction of balance in the issues of freedom and responsibility. Both M. Scott Peck and Victor Frankl are credited for these words:

> A *Statue of Responsibility* should be erected on the West Coast (of the U.S.) to serve as a balance to the *Statue of Liberty* on the East Coast.(3)

This statue is currently under construction. (visit www.statueofresponsibility.com)

Places Where We Fall as Small Communities, Clans and Cultures

As the circle widens including greater numbers of interconnected people, balance issues become more complex, but no less important. A group mentality soon emerges in every group. This mentality determines the course of the group as well as its imbalances. Imbalances common to clans, churches and small communities include inclusion versus exclusion; power versus principal; and progress versus compassion.

Inclusion versus Exclusion: Each group determines its standards of inclusion. Some are outwardly stated and easily understood. Kiwanis, Rotary, Jaycees and Kinsmen as well as many other social and civic clubs all have written, stated rules of membership and involvement. Clans, which tend to be more family or geographically oriented, do not typically have such written codes, although the code exists and is well known by most members! Churches and religious groups, and to a lesser degree all other groups, have both a written code as well as an unwritten code of membership.

Who is in and *who is out* is an issue of balance, although rarely considered in that light. Some groups wish to maximize membership; other groups wish to restrict it and often there are both elements in the same group! The dynamics are fairly simple. Every existing group has a limited potential for new members, although they are often reluctant to admit it. Each group has written or unwritten ideas, or both, about who they are willing to include and who they are not willing to include. Each group must maintain some degree of membership or the group cannot survive. It is here that balance enters the picture.

A church with an aging membership serves as a good example. Younger people with lots of active children create an interesting dilemma in an older church. Yes, these younger families are the future, and yes they will assure the continuance of the group, but they create problems that many older parishioners are not willing to accept. The issue of inclusion and exclusion becomes yet another place, where, without balance falling is certain.

Power versus Principle: Every church, clan, or small community has some degree of power. That power may take one of many forms, but it always exists. That same group also has certain principles by which it operates. These may be clearly delineated or never identified, yet they exist and wield influence. The issue of imbalance emerges as the powers of the group interface with the principles of the group. This is often a see-saw of struggle with potentially volatile results.

Power is found in money, strong personalities, cherished traditions, identified offices or anywhere there exists a need for the continuance of the status quo. Power is usually learned rather than taught. It is not printed in the membership manual although the principles of the group often are printed. Power alone is not inherently evil. Power which is not balanced by principle is the very essence of evil.

This issue of imbalance is often framed in *means and ends* terminology. When it is said that "the end justifies the means" it is simply another way of saying that an overweight of power (imbalance) over principle is necessary to achieve the desired results. Imbalance can exist in an over-valuation favoring principle: principles can become so rigid that power is unable to exert influence to do anything.

The ability to align power with principle is the greatest potential for good in our world. Wielding power apart from principle is the very essence of evil.

Expedience versus Compassion: It is doubtful that any organization exists to harm its members. However, the actions of any given group reflects an ongoing conflict regarding the use of its resources. The primary question is often reduced to the welfare of the organization or the welfare of the members. Expedience is a descriptor often used to determine the welfare of the group's survival or resources; compassion is a representative word which may be used to represent the welfare of individual members. No group is exempt from struggle in maintaining this precarious balance. Out of balance, even with good intentions, it is common to see groups who sacrifice the reason for their existence in order to finance their continuance.

It needs to be repeated again, but it must be expressed without questioning values or making judgments: **everybody falls.**

5. PLACES WHERE WE FALL AS CHRISTIANS AND CHURCHES

It is extremely important to remember that Christians and churches are entirely subject to all the imbalances previously described simply because Christians are humans and churches are organizations. The oversight of this simple fact is a source of serious imbalance in both. However, because of the nature of their existence as spiritual entities, Christians and churches have additional concerns which other persons and organizations do not face. Although the following are by no means an exhaustive list of imbalances faced by Christian persons and groups they do represent many primary concerns.

Sacred versus Secular: The struggle to balance the holy with the common, the sacred with the secular is an ongoing struggle which has existed as long as man has had any form of relationship with God. In any age or any era the opponents are lined up on both sides. The side which wins determines the nature of the church. This is true of individual congregations as well as the largest denominations.

The sacred/secular balance is not simply a church issue. Balancing the sacred and secular is played out politically in what is traditionally identified as Church versus State. The nature of this balance was a critical consideration in the formation of Canadian and American governments. Extremes, once again, are our teachers in the need for balance. When the state is all powerful, there is no place for religious freedom. Churches are closed or severely restricted, and the persecution of religious elements is common. When the church is all powerful it has tended historically to deny the same freedoms to those outside the church which the state denied to those within the church. Both church and state, however, provide essential elements to good governance. The struggle for this balance is played out politically every day in North America and around the world. To a large degree the quality of life in any society is dependent upon maintaining this delicate balance.

The sacred/secular balance is a major issue in public education. Only the most uninformed would assert that religion has no place in education. Religions have played a vital role in all cultures. However, balancing the practices of religion within a given system is a source of major conflict and division.

The church itself struggles constantly in this area also. Those who lean more heavily to the *sacred* contend that it is best to try to remove oneself and the church from the influences of the *unregenerate world* and to immerse oneself in the *sacred*. Those on the secular side contend that there is a real world which requires real answers to real problems. Losing sight of this truth is neither high nor holy. It is quite obvious that the truth lies between the extremes, but determining where to draw the lines is, once again, the nature of the struggle.

Faith and Works: In the New Testament, it is James who provides the context for this classical distinction of balance (James 2:14-26). Doing and believing are inextricably bound together. To separate them is to create dissonance and discord. But separate them we do.

This concern is unique to those groups with spiritual concerns. There are many who strongly contend for an entirely spiritual approach to every issue. Others argue that we must do more than pray and worship. We must also feed the hungry, clothe the naked and seek justice for the poor and oppressed. The pattern of Christ's life and ministry reveals a beautiful blending of spiritual awareness wedded to very earthly and human concerns.

This topic also enters largely into the differing theological stances regarding entry into the Kingdom of God. Denominationally, the church is divided upon this issue. At one extreme there are those who contend that Faith alone is the gateway to heaven. On the other extreme there are those who contend that Good Works alone will determine one's place in eternity. Most groups fall somewhere in the middle of these extremes. Each groups carries its own collection of scriptures which tend to support their particular position.

In contrast to these extremes, the life and actions of Christ reveal a beautiful blending of spiritual awareness wedded to very earthly and human concerns.

Trust versus Examination: Everything about the Christian faith involves trust. Without this basic element there is no faith and nothing to build faith upon. However, the wolf is often presented in sheep's clothing. Both Jesus and Paul were well aware of this danger and thus it behooves the Christian to balance faith with an eyes-open examination of the facts. This sounds much easier to do than it really is. Faith is just that: believing in something which is not always in agreement with the facts. However, all that glitters is not theological gold. Any *Faith* statement which is not in agreement with Biblical truth is erroneous. Biblical truth, however, is subject to broad interpretation. If this sounds complicated, be assured that it is, but be also assured that this balance must be pursued. Without this balance, followers are lead down dangerous and destructive trails and a spirit of doubt and fear dominates any hope for the wonderful gifts of faith to operate effectively.

Stop, Go, Wait: The decision making process that is required for change in any area is, for the Christian believer, a spiritual matter. When decision making is approached without regard for the Spirit's guidance, it is possible to make a very good and rational decision which is exactly opposite of God's desires. Therefore, wisdom and painful experience prompts the believer to make *stop, go, and wait* situations serious times of prayer and listening.

Most decisions have at least two dimensions which are equally critical. The first dimension is the one which usually receives the most attention. It has to do with right or wrong, good or bad, helpful or harmful. The second dimension is often even more important. This dimension involves time:

> *There is a time for everything, and a season for every activity under heaven.* (Ecclesiastes 3:1)

Every activity of living requires decision, and all these decisions can be condensed to these three possibilities: *stop, go, or wait*.

To become expert at this task would almost assure one of complete success in any possible venture. Conversely, a consistent failure of the *stop, go, wait* test would equally guarantee failure. It is not within the scope of this writing to explore the various means of seeking and pursuing the will of God. Many good resources exist to perform this task. What is important is for the disciple to understand the critical nature of the timing of God's purposes. There is no equal measure of balance in God's time from our perspective. We might have to stop (worrying, weighing and wondering) and wait twenty years to do something vital (go) that only takes ten minutes to complete. The balance is God's, but without it we are bound for frustration and failure.

Dependence, Independence, Interdependence: Like *stop, go, and wait, dependence, independence and interdependence* are tri-balance realities. In both of these cases, it is essential that a third element be included in the formula. Two elements are not adequate for balance. It would require a perfect human being to remain constantly balanced in all three areas. Each person is typically either over or under-weighted in this tri-balance necessity.

There are times when independence is essential. Only out of this strength is it possible to continue when one must go alone.

Simultaneously the Christian must develop an unshakeable sense of dependence fully recognizing that without the resources of divine strength there is no possibility of divine results.

At the same time the believer must function internally, as well as externally, in a state of interdependence in a give and take, swing and slide, dip and roll dance with all the rest of humanity, especially other Christians. The loss of this balance projects a false and unattainable bravado which appears extremely arrogant and aloof.

The task of integrating *dependence, independence, and interdependence* is an extremely arduous pursuit that requires life-long attention. I doubt that this discipline is ever achieved by any method other than trial and error. Sadly, many never comprehend the need for this tri-balance and live lives characterized by debilitating dependency or independent loneliness.

Task, Relationship: Many Christians are highly motivated. Some are driven. Both groups wish to perform certain tasks or reach certain goals. These are admirable traits but, when relationships hinder one's personal need to produce or achieve, conflict is inevitable.

Proponents line up on both sides of the fence, but this issue is particularly sticky in church matters because Christians are commanded by Christ to love each other (John 13:34), and Christians are also encouraged to work (Luke 10:2). People often get in the way of the work that individuals are intent upon doing. The result is obvious. Some Christians sacrifice their work in order to get along and be accepted; others run over as many people as necessary in order to get the work done. This continues as a never-ending battle among good, decent, well-intentioned persons. The solution is rarely simple or rapid. The pain and alienation from the battle often result in deep division and animosity.

The missing element is obviously a balance which considers the importance of the task as well the importance of the persons involved. Achieving this balance is an arduous never-ending task which requires tremendous energy, patience and love.

Liturgical Sacramental or Informal Spontaneous: Another battleground for the church exists in the tension created by differing approaches to the way *worship* is to be enacted. Some worshippers prefer rigidly structured experiences whereas others desire greater openness. Various opinions are usually stated with a flair of both rational and spiritual tones, although personal tastes are generally the issue at hand.

This issue has a strongly denominational flavor as well. Christian denominations are often characterized as liturgical or congregational. Implicit in this division is the somewhat misleading idea that the liturgical churches are very highly structured and rigorously organized whereas as the congregational style of Church is less structured and more *open*. These characteristics may vary widely from church to church within the denomination.

The real balance problem occurs within the organization itself where individuals want the church to move in one direction or another. It would be very convenient if every Christian had the same tastes in worship. It would also be very boring. This balance issue is not so much an issue of quality as it is an issue of power and needs to be recognized and dealt with as such.

Freedom, Order, and Structure (also Justice and Grace): To what degree is the church allowed to determine my actions and behavior? This is the primary question underlying the rocky ground of discussions regarding freedom, order and structure. Very strong opinions always emerge in discussions on this topic. One side would argue that the church has absolutely no right to expect anything of the Christian. These libertarians would insist that the Christian faith is completely private and nobody's business except that of the individual involved.

Others contend that belonging to the church is a life-long commitment and that this relationship is constantly open to review and scrutiny by other believers. Some churches remove people regularly from their rolls for violations of faith or practice. History has many examples of churches which operated with this assumption.

Persons on both sides of this issue would insist that this is not an issue of balance. However, the picture of the woman caught in adultery recorded in John 8:2-11 reminds us that God's laws and man's laws come together only in his Son. God chooses to relate to his children with an equal and balanced measure of both justice and grace. Either this balance is present or God has no part in the discussion.

Love the World, Love Not the World: Christians are encouraged not to love the world:

> *Do not love the world or anything in the world. If anyone loves the world, the love of the Father is not in him. For everything in the world— the cravings of sinful man, the lust of his eyes and the boasting of what he has and does—comes not from the Father but from the world.* (1 John 2:15-16)

But Christians are also told how much God loves the world:

> *For God so loved the world that he gave his one and only Son that whoever believes in him shall not perish but have eternal life.* (John 3:16)

The Greek word for world (cosmos) is the same word in both cases. This apparent contradiction has been a source of confusion and debate for centuries. There have been many Christian groups over the centuries who have identified their primary purpose to be removing themselves from the corruption of the world in order to move closer to God. Monasteries and convents, retreats and cathedrals have been built for this purpose. The Catholic Church has seen large orders which have functioned for centuries who have existed for the purpose of denying the *world*. Other groups have risen from many other denominations who have created cloisters and communes primarily for this purpose.

Other Christians find their calling directly related to the world and very much outside the Church. These Christians seek to care for and serve the world. Many are active in seeking to introduce the Gospel of Christ to those in the world. Every Christian person, group, order and denomination must continually face the tension of this reality and seek the balance of God's direction.

Jesus is the Answer, Jesus is the Problem: Christians struggle and often fall as a result of an imbalance in the application of the words and the teachings of Christ. In well-intentioned efforts to make the gospel more appealing to non-Christians the gospel is often presented as a quick and easy solution to all the problems of life. Thus, bumper stickers and church signs and promotional campaigns declare: "Jesus is the Answer!"

And, Jesus is the answer! Every Christian would confirm the truth of Jesus statement:

> *Jesus answered, "I am the way and the truth and the life. No one comes to the Father except through me. (John 14:6)*

The problem arises from the application of these words which give the hearer the impression that once you have become a Christian, your problems are over! In truth, when one becomes a Christian, the problems are just beginning! Jesus made it very clear that this was to be the case. In many places throughout the gospels Jesus candidly told his disciples that they must suffer just as He would suffer:

> *Brother will betray brother to death, and a father his child; children will rebel against their parents and have them put to death. All men will hate you because of me, but he who*

stands firm to the end will be saved. (Matthew 10:21-22)

When Christ is presented as the solution to every discomfort, disappointment is inevitable and many seekers choose to exit the gospel bus.

It is equally possible for Christians to become so focused on the difficulties they are facing that they become resentful and angry at God, church and others. Although it is rarely acknowledged, for these Christians, Jesus is the problem. It is also very common to become so caught up in dealing with life's problems that one may forget the resources of strength and encouragement which Christ offers to His brothers and sisters. J. I. Packer's book *Knowing God* has a superb chapter dealing with "These Inward Trials". This chapter is well worth the time required to read and study it.[1]

In conclusion, life for the Christian—as an individual disciple, as a member of a particular church and denomination, as a member of society who bears Christian values—is a daily challenge! It is impossible to face that challenge without the help of God in three persons: Father, Son and Spirit.

---

[1] In this volume, Packer also states on page 22 that "balanced" is a horrible, self-conscious word, although much of this work is Packer's effort to balance knowledge about God, which is essential, with a personal knowledge of God Himself. Packer is objecting to those who have knowledge apart from relationship. His objection to this use of the word is well taken.

Many voices say many things which do not agree. Balance is not easy to find or keep. But if balance is ignored or overlooked, one thing is certain:

You will return to the problem!

PART II:

FALLING INTO BALANCE

6. HOW DO WE KNOW WHEN A WRECK IS ON THE WAY?

Balance can be carried too far. There is no *balance* when it comes to murder, theft, adultery or anything else which is intrinsically destructive. Some people claim to be balanced when they are only unzipped. It is virtually impossible to speak of balance apart from values. For many persons, values are entirely personal and self-determined. Others maintain a very rigid set of values which they rigorously seek to impose upon themselves and every other person.

It is only fair and appropriate to attempt to identify some of my bias as author of this book, recognizing that all values are biased approaches to life. My values emerge from an opinionated but somewhat informed understanding of the Bible, the scriptures of the Christian faith. I am further biased by a lifetime of immersion in Evangelical and, much later, Charismatic theology. To state otherwise would destroy any credibility I might have attained to address this subject. Allow me to belabor the point.

We can never hope to achieve the life-giving benefits of the pursuit of balance until we are willing to identify and understand our own inherent slant or bias to everything we encounter.

> At the root of most communication problems are perception or credibility problems. None

of us see the world as it is but as we are, as our frames of reference, or *maps* define the territory. And our experience-induced perceptions greatly influence our feelings, beliefs, and behavior. (5)

It is not the intended purpose of this writing to *balance* the reader to my biased thinking. It is the intent of this book to challenge reader and writer to examine individual bias, to see both sides of the complex issues of life from a Biblical perspective and to seek the positive rewards of this often painful investigation. All of this is simply a long way of defining balance in a perspective which I hope will prove beneficial.

Every person and every group is unique and has differing structures. Regardless of one's starting point, however, there comes a time in the life of every person, every family, every business and church and organization when the wheels are off the tracks and the wreck has occurred. At some time before that fatal moment, things started to wobble and vibrate. Strange noises, starting small and growing louder, began their insistent cry of imminent warning. Very unpleasant smells and quite probably smoke begins to appear in unlikely or unseen places. Although the signs are there, they are often ignored. Disaster is imminent. Somebody needs to stop the train! Some individual or group of individuals need to know when balance is being compromised.

How do we know when we are losing our balance?

Before we can answer this vital question, it is important to recognize that there are forces at work resisting balance. There are other forces that directly oppose it. Without trying to create another *conspiracy theory*, it is necessary for us to recognize that these forces work to sabotage the existence and continuation of existing balance.

What kind of forces are likely to sabotage balance? Any force which carries a personal interest that is greater than its concern for the whole is capable of sabotage. Some of these interests include:

- maintaining the status quo

- pushing forward a special agenda

- seeking to discredit something which is operating in the system

- seeking to elevate someone or something to a greater place of power

In addition, there are some interests, sadly enough, whose only purpose is to destroy the entire system.

It does not take a great deal of imagination to see how these sabotage attempts play themselves out. What is very hard to see is how we play a part in this conspiracy.

Let's take a far-flung example which illustrates the point:

> Joe Big decides he wants to have the strongest right arm in the world. Joe goes to work. He devotes hours and days; he sweats and agonizes; he pushes himself; his right arm starts to grow. At first, the rest of Joe's body and the rest of Joe's world begin to make some quiet mutterings. Left arm feeling a little *left out* starts to slowly withdraw. Joe's wife who likes to encourage Joe in his

pursuits only makes a few remarks regarding Joe's absence and focus. Time goes on. Joe's right arm really starts to grow. Joe enters a local *Strong Arm Contest* and wins the contest hands down! Joe is approached by a strong-arm-promoter who promises to take Joe to the *strong arm big time*. Both Joe's arm and his head begin to grow.

Meanwhile, Joe's back begins to complain. Joe's back cannot help but see how its load has increased tremendously and begins to ask itself: "Just how far am I willing to go?" Joe's left arm, now half it's original size, grows even smaller. His left arm cannot help but remember the good old days when it had as much value as the right arm. Joe's legs begin to ache as a result of hour after hour of sitting and almost no walking at all. One of the legs even mentions the dreaded *s* word: who knows if a *strike* can be avoided?

Joe's wife, once supportive, has grown bitter and resentful. "All he cares about is his stupid arm!" She grudgingly decides that it is time to fight fire with fire. She is going to hire a divorce lawyer to scare Joe into rethinking this whole strong arm venture. If threats are not effective, she is thinking she may have to carry through with her threat and pursue the divorce.

We know that we are losing balance when life is no longer manageable, rewarding, or fun -- when our purpose is unclear and our efforts are tedious rather than fulfilling. In essence when we lose our joy we have lost our balance.

When life is not manageable we have lost control. Things outside of our intentions, goals or even desires have started running the machine of our existence. When life is no longer rewarding, we continue to do the same amount of work with little or no sense of purpose or accomplishment. Every adult recognizes that fun is not part of all activities, but when daily existence is devoid of joy and laughter, it is very good sign that something is out of whack.

In the case of Joe Big, what could have made the difference? What clues did Joe miss? There is nothing inherently wrong with developing one's strength. It is very easy for Joe to simply say that no one understands him, and that his pursuit of excellence is worth any cost. Many speakers and writers agree with Joe. Many athletes, aspiring business leaders, politicians, clergy, even parents are driven by the pursuit of excellence. This pursuit is admirable and achieves significant results, but only for a brief period of time.

Balance becomes an issue any time the costs of our pursuits is greater than the sum of our reward.

At first thought, the previous statement seems coldly selfish, and it can be. Far too often, however, we live our days unaware of either what we want or what it will cost us to get it. Unless there is a specific determined thought and prayer process, most of life is a series of reactions to whatever threatens or soothes our daily impulses. Those who seek to live their lives completely focused on goals and objectives face another dilemma. When anything takes our time, it is taking our life. What goals and objectives are worth the sacrifice of one's life?

Balance is uniquely personal. No other human in all the universe can tell you how to balance your life. But God can! Because he is Creator, God can show his creatures how to make their engines work. It may sound too patronizing or directive for some, but I will say it anyway:

> **Only the designer and creator
> can fully explain
> or repair the mechanism.
> And, when we are not
> in ongoing consultation
> with the one who made us,
> the wheels are coming off.**

7. THE CHRIST LIFE: A MODEL OF BALANCE

Jesus went through all the towns and villages, teaching in their synagogues, preaching the good news of the kingdom and healing every disease and sickness. (Matthew 9:35)

Jesus focused his time upon teaching and preaching and healing. These were his undisputed priorities. Each priority was equally important. He was intent upon announcing and ushering in the Kingdom of God. He saw with burning clarity that every living person needed to know the good news of the kingdom of God in order to avoid experiencing the reality of separation in hell. He was no less passionate about teaching the nature of the new covenant that his Father was beginning in Him. Moved with compassion for the needs of the multitudes, he healed the sick, raised the dead and fed the hungry.

Matthew 9:35 is a magnificent verse which superbly summarizes everything that Christ was and everything he aspired to do. If any part of this verse is absent, an inadequate picture of Jesus is the inevitable result.

Jesus Christ is the world's best example of human living. He holds this distinction largely because of his unique ability to balance life's most significant priorities. It can be argued that the very nature of sin is the innate inability to find and follow the critical balances required for meaningful living. The unguided human condition always tends to extremes rather than balance. We are far more prone to eat too much chocolate rather than not enough. In fact, balance may seem at times to be an impossible goal, a pipe-dream only appearing in a philosopher's imagination. There is only one example in all of mankind's history of a truly balanced life. There have been many lives well worth emulating, but only one who ever lived in perfect balance.

Hebrews 4:15 declares Jesus' sinless life. This is rarely connected with the divine ability to maintain the balance necessary to make a sinless life possible. As we inventory the balances which Jesus maintained, this truth becomes more and more apparent. Jesus Christ maintained distinctive and noteworthy balance in these areas:

Jesus was Divine and Human: A discussion of Jesus' balance must begin with the only challenge that has never confronted any other person. Jesus Christ was both Man and God. If he had not lived this aspect of his life in perfect balance, he would have created far more confusion than light, and we would have been left with an entirely different image of God. The first major disagreements within the Christian church developed into international conflicts later called councils, which were concerned with this primary issue. The church has never faced a more critical subject, then or now. The question seems unimportant until one begins to grasp the consequence of an unbalanced Jesus in the matter of his divine/human nature. If Jesus had been *more God than man*, we would not have a "great high priest who has been tempted in all manner as we have yet was without sin" (Hebrews 4:15). We would not enjoy the tremendous understanding and care of one who has walked every road of human suffering, except the road of sin.

If Jesus had been *more man than God*, humans would not have access to the power to change what man cannot change. It is truly wonderful to have a friend, but in life's eternal issues, a friend is not enough. We need divine help. We need more than encouragement. We need a Savior!

No other human who ever lives will have to face this particular issue of balance. Only Christ confronted this challenge. However, it is critical for his followers to understand that his faithfulness in balancing these two aspects of his life have opened the doors for each of us to pursue his life of balance as well. Without his faithfulness in this area, a balanced life would be beyond hope.

Now we focus on those areas in which we also struggle with balance:

Jesus projected Severe Austerity and Comforting Warmth: True to the nature of His father, Jesus Christ exhibits an amazing capacity for both extreme austerity and amazing affection. Contrast the difference between Jesus' dealings with the Pharisees and his dealings with little children. Confronted with the force of religious hypocrisy, Jesus was ruthless. In Matthew 23:13-36, Jesus calls the Pharisees hypocrites, blind guides, whitewashed tombs, snakes, and a brood of vipers. One can only imagine the force of the Son of God in these accusations. Unbridled raw divine power was apparent and undoubtedly the Pharisees recognized it! This same power was present as Jesus drove the merchants and money changers from the temple (Matthew 21, Mark 11, and Luke 19).

In stark contrast, Matthew (12:20) quotes Isaiah (42:3) in describing Jesus in this manner:

> *A bruised reed he will not break, and a smoldering wick he will not snuff out, till he leads justice to victory.*

Gentle, meek, mild, warm, caring, compassionate, forgiving, kind, warm: all are appropriate words to describe Him. Jesus was greatly drawn to children, and children were greatly drawn to Him. Children are usually great judges of inner intent, and they flocked to Jesus. The disciples felt compelled to try to stop them but Jesus said.

> *Suffer the little children to come to me.* (Matthew 19:14)

Jesus reflects perfectly the nature of his Father in exhibiting a nature of both divine wrath and divine compassion. The human tendency is to gravitate toward a God of love not a God of wrath. Thus, we create the God we want rather than the God who is.

Jesus balanced the Demands of Family with the Call of God: The Bible provides only sketchy details of the early life of Christ. His earthly father, Joseph, so prominent in his birth, is absent during his adult years. It is reasonable to assume Joseph's death. One can only speculate what a difference Joseph's death made in the life his family. Jesus was the elder son. Upon the death of the father, the elder son became the head of the family. Assuming this responsibility would have made it impossible for Jesus to pursue the call of God. The manner in which he approached this difficulty is highly instructive.

Being the head of a Jewish family was a very good thing. It was a cultural necessity. For thirty years of his life, Jesus lived in the fullest compliance of that expectation. Then came the day when the Spirit said it was time for Jesus to pursue God's agenda. Undoubtedly, Jesus loved his mother very deeply. This is most clearly revealed at the cross as he places her in John's care, although one would question how his brothers and sisters would view such an action. We know almost nothing of his relationship with his half siblings. Some scholars (6) argue quite convincingly that the siblings identified in Matthew 13:55 (James, Joseph, Simon, and Judas and "all his sisters") may be cousins or very close relatives which would allow Mary, Jesus' mother, to be the perpetual virgin as some Roman Catholics contend. Others suggest that these mentioned were Mary's children born naturally by Joseph.

In either case, what is perfectly clear is that until his death, Jesus' siblings did not accept him as Messiah or believe that he was in his right mind (7) Jealousy may have played a vital part. After his death, but not before, there is some indication that they believed in him as the Messiah.(8)

Perhaps the key passage regarding Jesus relationship with his family is Matthew 12: 46-50, which is paralleled in Mark 3 and Luke 8. In these scriptures, after he is told that his mother and brothers wished to speak to him, Jesus identifies his mother and brothers as those who do the will of his Father in heaven. He identified his true family—which did not necessarily exclude his (quasi) genetic family. Undoubtedly there were those who did not understand. Jesus died at great odds with the members of his immediate family.

One often finds himself/herself at odds with family expectations. It is utterly impossible to meet the many and varied demands of family. Those who try, often encounter incredible frustration. Abandonment of the family is equally undesirable and always detrimental. In

1 Timothy 5:8, Paul calls such a person worse than an unbeliever.

So what made Jesus' family dynamics a model of balance? Two things:

- Jesus did not allow family or cultural expectations to deter him from wholeheartedly obeying His Heavenly Father

- Jesus never lost sight of the need to care for his family as he was given opportunity

Contrast Jesus words in Luke 14:26 with his words in John19:27. How can anyone in his right mind say that "those who come after him must hate one's father and mother...or he cannot be my disciple" and later, in his dying moments of excruciating pain, seek to secure his dearest friend's assistance in providing for his mother's care? These irreconcilable statements are a reflection of the tension experienced by every follower of Christ. It is not easy to balance family and God's call, but it is essential and it pleases God. Maintaining this aspect of a balanced life did not endear Christ either to his family or his followers. But it did please God, because God deeply cares about both.

Jesus balanced Labor and Rest: In the matter of labor and rest, Jesus is an obedient reflection of his Father God. Inherent to the Ten Commandments is a divine directive to maintain this balance. From the beginning, God has seen rest and work, in balance, as an inherent part of productive living. From the beginning, mankind has found it almost impossible to maintain this balance. The Sabbath commandment in Jesus' day had become a rule to be kept rather than a blessing to be enjoyed. Jesus' contribution in this area was to balance the rule-keeping with the commandment's original intent. He ran head-on into the path of the rule-keepers who ultimately demanded his death. It is interesting to recognize that it is very easy to gather group consensus for the making of rules, and almost impossible to gain group consensus when seeking balance.

Parallel to this discussion is the recognition that the *Christ presence* always brings to any concern the balance of God's intent versus culture's propensity for rule making. Cultural rules so quickly turn 180 degrees from the creator's original intent, turning something really good into something very destructive.

In Mark 2:27, Jesus reminded his hearers that the Sabbath was made for man and not man for the Sabbath. Was the Sabbath important? Absolutely! Was work important? Absolutely! Was the cart ahead of the horse? Undoubtedly.

The presence of Christ has the ability to bring the Father's perspective to each and every conflict between rules and relationships. Try as we may, human wisdom rarely succeeds in bringing this balance.

Jesus balanced Work and Play: The record of Jesus' life does not include an instance which identifies Jesus' playing a game or pursuing a hobby. There is not a verse which says "Jesus laughed", although we are very familiar with the verse which says "Jesus wept"(John 11:35). In Jesus' life we see numerous instances which can be readily identified as work. But where is the play, the recreation, the fun in this man of sacred balance?

In the absence of direct comments such as *Jesus played*, the Bible leaves us with the record of a man's life which reveals a person of great joy. Yes, Isaiah 53:3 clearly states "he was a man of sorrow, acquainted with grief", but the record reveals so much more.

Perhaps the greatest proof of Jesus' joyous, even playful personality, is the Bible's record of Jesus and children. **Jesus was an honest-to-goodness *kid magnet*!** No other Bible character even comes close to Jesus when it came to children. Interestingly, one day some rowdy children were scornfully jeering the prophet Elisha along and kept calling him a *baldhead.* The scripture says that Elisha brought down a curse from the Lord on them: two bears came and mauled forty-two of the youths!(9)

Unlike Elisha, children were magnetically drawn to Jesus. Little people frequently surrounded the Son of God. Parents brought them to Jesus for his blessing. The disciples thought they were in the way, and received his rebuke. Certain Pharisees were angry that children were shouting *Hosanna to the son of David* in the temple area after Jesus had cleared the temple of merchants and healed the lame and blind. (10) Children have not changed. They are inevitably drawn to a person who knows how to stop and see and laugh and play.

Humour is subject to time and change. Circumstance and situation may make some things appear humorous at the time, but humour rarely lasts the moment. It is widely believed that Jesus used a great deal of humour in his teaching although this is difficult to document especially because we do not live in first-century Palestine. Elton Trueblood listed thirty stories Jesus told that make their point with humour. (11) I think Jesus laughed a lot or he would have never made it to the cross.

Did Jesus ever take a vacation? Did he ever celebrate a holiday? The answer is a definite yes. The only incident recorded in Jesus' teen years happened when his family was on *vacation.* The feast of the Passover was an integral part of Jewish life and it combined religious ceremony with a break from work and a trip with family and friends to the big city. On this trip, Joseph and Mary traveled an entire day until they became concerned that Jesus was missing from their group. Three days later(!) they found him, having fun in the temple talking to and confounding the elders with his wisdom. Like a normal teen, he could not believe his absence was a big deal.

Periodically Jesus took his disciples to places of rest. His entire ministry had something of an adventurous air about it. There were no predetermined schedules which had to be met: no planes or buses to catch, no time clocks that had to be punched and part of the cost for this experience was donated by a number of women. (12) There were, however, many long and stressful days filled with crowds of people carrying monstrous needs. These days took their toll even upon the son of God. Mark and Matthew record an incident in the region of Tyre, a Philistine city whose citizens were *Canaanites*. To the Jewish mind this equated them with the lowest of pagans. The scripture tells us,

> *He entered a house and did not want anyone to know it; yet he could not keep his presence secret.* (Mark 7:24)

Jesus, under the pressure of constant assault by Jewish Pharisees, the incessantly curious, and others in desperate need, took his disciples out of the country for *R and R*. We have no idea how long they stayed and only one incident is recorded, but the point is clear: Jesus went there for a break before returning to the demands which awaited him.

The son of God came to earth with the most important job in all of history to perform. He still had time to laugh and play with little children. A better picture of balance does not exist.

Jesus balanced the Sacred and the Secular, the Physical and the Spiritual: It is just as possible for the *Saint* to be so heavenly-minded that he is of no earthly good, as it is for the *Sinner* to be so earthly-minded that he has no heavenly hope. Jesus was earthly-minded enough to know the reality of physical needs and heavenly-minded enough not to focus his whole being upon the never-ending demands of needy persons.

The Son of God was born to what was probably a lower middle class family who had to deal with all the struggles of daily survival. As the eldest child of a carpenter, Jesus was not allowed the luxury of focusing exclusively on spiritual matters. Undoubtedly he had to learn to clean the shop, care for the garbage, carry the wood and water and do the daily chores he was assigned-- just like everybody else. He was not exempted from work because he was holy.

Undoubtedly, he heard his fair share of gossip, profanity and lurid stories just like every other carpenter's kid. Surely there were times when business was slow or Dad was sick when family had to make do with what they had. There were probably times when hunger was all too close. We do not know these truths because the Bible records them, but because we know that Jesus entered this kind of world. Therefore, part of the explanation for Jesus ability to balance the sacred and the secular is a result of the fact that God planned a childhood experience for his Son in rural Nazareth as the eldest son of a Galilean tradesman.

The child of very wealthy parents is not particularly impressed by large cathedrals or places of worship. Such things are common in his/her world, although that child may certainly develop an appreciation for holy things. A child of poor parents may be awed by tremendous structures and yet never gain a sense of holiness. Balancing sacred and secular is more than education or wealth. It is more than culture, theology or liturgy. In common with all the balances one must seek, balancing the sacred with the secular is a gift of God himself. The same God who made the magnificence of the aurora borealis also made animals with bowel movements. To focus on one to the exclusion of the other is to miss the mystery of God.

Jesus walked. He walked everywhere he went. Only once is he seen riding, and this time it was an apparently unbroken colt of a donkey. This trusty steed was very small, very slow, and very unimpressive. A conquering hero entering a city rode a white horse. Jesus rode a half-grown ass. When one walks as much as Jesus did, he learns the road intimately. Jesus walked through dry, hot, dusty, stretches of road that sometimes were deep sand and other times filled with rocks. Upon occasion the road turned to mud, possibly snow and ice, but he wore only sandals, no Nikes. In the city he walked through garbage and manure on the same roads the animals traveled. When one walks in desert regions, thirst is not an academic subject. Water had to be carried by the traveler. The Messiah's means of travel dictated a constant reminder of the very real *secular* needs of his world. Sick people followed him constantly. Many followed him because they were hungry for food. Others were hungry for a word from God. He fed both hungers.

In contrast to Jesus' immersion in the real physical world, we observe his abiding love for His Father's house, the Temple of Jerusalem. This love went all the way back to his childhood. His deep love and care for God's temple is seen graphically as all four gospels record at least one event (perhaps more) when Jesus threw out money changers and merchants from the temple. Jesus speaks

> *It is written, my house will be called a house of prayer, but you are making it a den of robbers.* (Matthew 21:13)

> *His disciples remembered that it is written: "Zeal for your house will consume me."* (Psalm 69:9; John 2:17)

The *sacred and secular* issue was directly confronted again when Jesus addressed the Pharisees with their objections to healing on the Sabbath. Jesus' purpose was not to desecrate the sacredness of the Sabbath. His purpose was to reveal the caring heart of Jehovah God for those in great physical need:

> *Now if a child can be circumcised on the Sabbath so that the law of Moses may not be broken, why are you angry with me for healing the whole man on the Sabbath? Stop judging by mere appearances and make a right judgment.* (John 7:23)

Perhaps the greatest challenge faced by the early church centered around this issue. This issue was the burning question which prompted the first great Council of the church in Nicaea in 325 A.D. In the first three centuries (and still today) many persuasive voices taught that Jesus was the Son of God but he was not a man. He was not born as a human, they say, because the world is evil and God did not create an evil world. Therefore, Jesus was God but not man. He was not incarnate; he had not been born to a virgin; he did not experience life as humans experience it.

Even after his resurrection Christ is observed, not as a spirit, but as a recognizable human being. He directed Thomas to put his finger in the nail prints of his hand. He made breakfast for Peter and other disciples by the sea of Galilee and he ate with them. He was seen and recognized for a period of forty days after his resurrection. (13)

In view of these events we see a picture of Jesus' life walking a carefully laid tightrope that spans the divide between the holy and the common, between the sacred and the earthly, and between the physical and the spiritual. And we see the Son of God walking this balance superbly well. The apostle Paul says it well:

> *For we do not have a great high priest who is unable to sympathize with us in our weaknesses, but we have one who was tempted in every way, just as we are--yet without sin. Let us then approach the throne of grace with confidence, so that we may receive mercy and find grace to help in time of need.* (Hebrews 4:15-16)

Jesus balanced being a Recluse and an Activist: Christians leaders, followers and writers often fall in one of two categories. These categories have many names. On the one side there are those who see the Faith lived out most effectively in quiet retreat, solitude, deep contemplation and in pursuit of mystical experience. These Christians focus upon an inner journey aspiring to a closer relationship and greater obedience to Christ. Others Christians pursue similar goals in different directions seeing the Christian life as a hands-on, day-by-day reality that is best lived in the midst of the greatest human activity. Both groups function primarily upon the assumption that true holiness emerges most effectively by following their predetermined path. Personality is usually the primary factor in this choice. Individuals lean toward extrovert or introvert tendencies. At the risk of sounding trite or repetitive, Jesus was both. We can readily see that the son of God exhibited distinct traits which give credence to both approaches in the pursuit of holiness.

The Lord Jesus Christ was no stranger to the inner journey. He did nothing publicly until he was thirty years old. Following his baptism by John, the Spirit of God led him to enter the desert for a period of forty days of fasting. There, he was specifically tempted by Satan to be something less than God had planned for him to be. Over and over the disciples record that he would exit the company of others to seek solitude in places of quiet and meditation. Jesus' travels were not dictated by a rigid itinerary taking him to strategic places of power. He seemed to be rambling rather than advancing. He seemed just as concerned with the water stops and the children on the way as he was with delivering sermons in the synagogue.

Had Jesus lived to reach old age we would have a better picture of the stark contrast between retreat and confrontation. We have no way of knowing what later years would have revealed in any part of His life, but especially in this area. Given the shortness of his life, it is amazing that this contrast is so apparent. It is extremely informative to recognize the powerful influence of the multiple orders, societies, brotherhoods, schools, monasteries and, to some degree, even denominations which have leaned to one side or the other of this aspect of Jesus life.

There is only one way to see the Christ. He is forever found right in the center of everything that is God-pleasing and life-affirming, and He is always separate and apart from anything that is not. And that is divine balance.

Jesus balanced being Evangelist and Caregiver: The Church, the Body of Christ, is divided on many lines. A prominent division is the *E- division*. Many churches and even denominations choose to align themselves with other churches that see themselves as either *Evangelical* or *Ecumenical* or *Eucharistic*. Typically, *Eucharistic* churches focus their activities around the sacraments. *Evangelical* churches supposedly focus on inviting non-believers to become Christians. *Ecumenists* focus on bringing Christian groups to greater harmony with one another. Some churches focus on the physical needs of a suffering world while other groups focus on spiritual needs. There is no real consensus among these groups on exactly what the *"E"* words mean because each group typically interprets these words from their own unique perspective. Therefore, there is usually greater agreement within each group as to what it is not, rather than what it is.

This division is far from God's intention for the working of His church. God's agenda revealed by Christ's life did not limit itself to *either/or* guidelines. God's purpose has always been to care for the needs of the whole person: body, soul, spirit; physical, mental and spiritual; mind, heart, and psyche; lock, stock and barrel. Any ministry that focuses only on one of these needs will always fall short of God's intentions.

Many gifted individuals and groups and even denominations do certain things extremely well. Usually, there are many other things which they do not do very well at all. God, in His infinite wisdom, does not give it all to any person or any organization. God's plan is designed so that we must work together, relying upon one another, to see His will accomplished.

Jesus, unlike other persons or organizations, was gifted to bring all of his Father's heart to the table. Christ brings both the good news (evangelism) along with the good work (care giver). *Eucharistic, Ecumenism,* and *Evangelism,* are beautiful words which cannot be uttered in isolation by those who seek to follow Him.

Jesus Balanced Poverty and Wealth: Scriptures help us to see Jesus as both rich and poor, very wealthy and having very little. Often He is portrayed as one or the other—which is a direct contradiction of the life that the scriptures portray. Look at the record. as he spoke to a would-be disciple:

> *Foxes have holes and birds have nests, but the Son of Man does not have a place to lay his head.* (Matthew 8:20)

> *In my Fathers house are many rooms; if it were not so, I would have told you. I am going there to prepare a place for you.* (John 14:2)

He is not identified as owning anything except the clothes he wore. Speaking of his clothes, some make the case that his coat/cloak was of such great value that the soldiers at the foot of the cross wanted it enough to gamble for it. These argue that no one in poverty would own such as coat. A number of women, obviously of considerable means, chose to support his ministry. When he was pressed by Peter for money to pay the temple tax, He directed him to go catch a fish which would have a coin in his mouth (just enough to cover the tax). Jesus grew up in Nazareth, a remote village of such little consequence that Nathaniel asked:

Indeed, can anything good come from Nazareth? (John 1:46)

Others have contended that as a carpenter he was a well-to-do member of that culture.

One cannot read these accounts without a recognition of Jesus' royalty transposed beside his obscurity. It was both mockery and unparalleled honor when the sign was placed on the cross reading *King of the Jews*.(14)

Jesus often spoke of the deceitfulness and danger of riches, but he was never stingy or miserly with his desire to give food to the hungry or healing to the sick and never worried about his supplies running out. We have not one indication that Jesus ever lacked anything he needed to do what he wished to do. It would appear that He never bought a house or a cow or a piece of land, but he never criticized anyone for doing so. Jesus associated with some of the wealthiest in his society and, in Matthew 9, it is reported that he was criticized for these associations. Simultaneously he was just as quick to touch and heal a leper, a woman with a continuous flow of blood, and a crazy man running naked through the tombstones. It is virtually impossible to take the life of Christ and exalt poverty or riches as *Christ-like*. *Christ-like* is offering what one has to the glory of God.

It seems to be in the very nature of human DNA to associate either wealth or the lack of it with evil. The Son of God stands above this major source of war, murder, guilt, judgment and destruction to declare that His Father is the giver of all good gifts. To focus on the stuff apart from Giver is to fall headlong into one of Satan's finest traps.

Jesus balanced being both King and Servant: The son of God was both the greatest example of royal humility and servant supremacy. This truth is foreshadowed by the prophecies in Isaiah 52-53, regarding his coming. The circumstances surrounding his birth, his childhood and youth reveal royalty inherent in humble surroundings. The events of his crucifixion, death, and resurrection illustrate this powerful dichotomy.

The prophesies of the Old Testament regarding the anticipated Messiah wound together the threads of *King* and *Servant*. Isaiah describes the Messiah:

> *He had no beauty or majesty to attract us to him, nothing in his appearance that we should desire him.* (Isaiah 53:2)

Despised and rejected by men, a man of sorrows, familiar with suffering, like one from whom men hide their faces, despised and we esteemed him not: these are not thoughts typically associated with royalty.

> *After the suffering of his soul, he will see the light of life and be satisfied; by his knowledge my righteous servant will justify many, and he will bear their iniquities. Therefore I will give him a portion among the great, and he will divide the spoils with the strong, because he poured out his life unto death, and was numbered with the transgressors. For he bore the sin of many, and made intercession for the transgressors.* (Isaiah 53:11-12)

The servant/king contrast is also obvious in the birth of Messiah. This child destined to born in a stable to an unwed mother accompanied by her very uncertain and bewildered husband was welcomed and celebrated by unnumbered billions of heavenly hosts. This cosmic birth was eagerly sought by travelers bringing gifts from other nations in search of the Holy One and was feared enough by a reigning ruler to order the execution of any child who might be the One. These facts testify to the amazing contrast brought together by the servant king.

Everything about this man gave evidence of a contrast the world has found very frustrating. Jesus rode an ass's colt, not a white horse, into Jerusalem and the people honored him like a conquering hero. Jesus was crucified between two criminals, yet Pilate insisted that a sign be placed upon his cross identifying Jesus as *King of the Jews*. The world is still confused by such a King.

Jesus balanced Strength and Weakness (Meekness/Humility with Confidence/Power): An integral part of discerning balance in any area has to do with words and their meanings. The scriptures are entirely comfortable identifying Jesus as a person of humility. The exact opposite of humility is usually identified as prideful. *Prideful* is not a fitting word to describe Messiah. However, the picture rightly given of a *suffering servant* does not equate to a powerless servant. Describing Christ in terms of humility does not limit or diminish His strength.

Some of Jesus' actions were considered far enough removed from humility to be seen as ruthless. When he drove the merchants from the temple, *humble* is not one of the words used to describe his actions. When he told Pontius Pilate that he was indeed King of the Jews and earlier told Simon Peter that he could call twelve legions of angels to come to his aid if he chose to do so (Matthew 26 and 27), Jesus was displaying what some identified as extreme arrogance or downright blasphemy. When he calmed the storms of Galilee or quieted the Gadarene running naked among the tombstones and when he fed the thousands and commanded the demons not to identify him, Jesus displayed physical and spiritual power unparalleled in human experience. Isaiah gave a description of his actions:

> *Surely he took up our infirmities and carried our sorrows, yet we considered him stricken by God, smitten by him, and afflicted. But he was pierced for our transgressions, he was crushed for our iniquities; the punishment that brought us peace was upon him, and by his wounds we are healed.* (Isaiah 53:4-5)

> *A bruised reed he will not break, and a smoldering wick he will not snuff out. In faithfulness he will bring forth justice.* (Isaiah 42:3)

Jesus in his humiliation exhibited power beyond any human measurement. For finite minds it is almost impossible to separate meekness from weakness. In God's mind, weakness is the unparalleled source of strength. Grasping the nature of the Holy One requires at least a portion of the mind of God. Here, through God's eyes, we see this amazing amalgamation: utter humility and unlimited strength

Jesus balanced Authority and Submission: The strength of Jesus' authority was apparent to both friend and foe. The Gospels note particularly that he did not speak as the Scribes spoke, but as one with authority. This power was apparent to the twelve. They were convinced he was about to overthrow the Roman government and return Palestine to the glory of the days of David. The twelve disciples repeatedly displayed a struggle for leadership within the group. To them, as to us, power and position were inseparable. Their distinct ambitions are not identified. It is not entirely clear how Peter, James and John became something of an inner circle. They were present when Jesus spoke to Moses and Elijah. He asked them to pray for Him in the garden the night before he was arrested. Perhaps they were not chosen for these events, but were simply the ones willing to go. One cannot be sure. We do know that no disciple was given distinct *authority* except Judas Iscariot who was made responsible for dispensing finances for the group.

The struggle for power surfaced regularly. This power struggle climaxed when the mother of James and John requested that her sons be given the first and second places of command in Jesus *kingdom*. In this context, a minor squabble among unknown Palestinian ambitions, Jesus established the benchmark for leadership of every kind in every situation for all of time:

> *He that would be great among you must become servant of all.* (Mark 9:35)

Greatness and servitude are not commonly sought or joined. Jesus' actions illustrated the force of his teaching. Isaiah identifies the Messiah as suffering servant. The imagery was not new, but it took the Son of God to bring it to its pinnacle.

Pure raw ambition resides in some with greater intensity than others. Most of us desire to be at the head of the line. There are many who want to be in charge and few who want to clean up. Jesus made it clear that he was in full and complete obedience to His Father. He insisted that he did nothing on his own but only what his Father desired. He also made it clear that his Father was King above all Kings. Everything the Son did was in complete submission to his Father. Jesus was also in submission to certain humans and to all humans in a larger sense. Jesus requested Baptism of John, although John recognized that he needed the baptism of Christ. At the table of the last supper Messiah chose to wash the feet of his disciples as an act of utter submission.

Jesus was never invited to dine with royalty. He was never offered a job, a position or a title. He never got a salary, a pension, or a gold watch. What he did receive was ridicule, torture, and death. Just before his death he also received a sign which was placed on his cross:

Jesus of Nazareth: King of the Jews

On the cross against the skyline of that infamous day we see both tremendous irony and awesome majesty:

King of all Kings: Faithful Servant

Sacred balance.

Jesus balanced Suffering with Joy: It takes no imagination whatsoever to see the suffering of Jesus. Isaiah and four Gospel accounts graphically record the physical suffering which Christ experienced. Not so obvious is His emotional suffering, although we have glimpses, particularly in Gethsemane, before he was arrested. The greatest suffering we cannot truly comprehend at all. As the Lamb of God, the Incarnate Christ took upon himself the sins of all persons of all time.

As horrible as the crucifixion was, other persons have endured physical and emotional torture equal to and greater than the Christ. However, no one has ever conceived, much less experienced, the sacrifice and separation from God which the Son encountered. No one else has borne the sins of mankind. No wonder Isaiah identifies Messiah as *a man of sorrows, acquainted with grief.*

Seeing the joy of Jesus is not so readily apparent. In the gospels we read "Jesus wept" but we do not read "Jesus laughed". We do not read, "Jesus smiled." Some have concluded that Jesus was the ultimate killjoy. Algernon Swinburne, in his "Hymn to Prospernine" wrote the following:

> Thou hast conquered O' pale Galilean,
> the world has grown gray from thy breath.

These words summarize the attitude of many that the only Christian colors are gray and black.

The writer of Hebrews presents another intriguing perspective:

> *Let us fix our eyes upon Jesus the author and perfecter of our faith, who for the joy set before him endured the cross scorning its shame and sat down at the right hand of the throne of God.* (Hebrews 12:2)

What is this *joy set before him?* Our Messiah took joy in giving what no one else could give. The cross was the only road to man's redemption. The cross was a tremendous price to pay. Although some were consumed with grief, not a single *Thank You* was uttered. But the joy was there. Without it, the Son of God could find nothing on which to hang his hurt.

The evidence of joy permeates the accounts of Messiah's life. We have already noted the tremendous attraction which children displayed for Jesus. How many joyless people are able to attract children? Scriptures indicate that, when they were invited, some of the disciples simply dropped what they were doing to follow Jesus, the teacher. The Pharisees were very distressed that Jesus spent so much time with *sinners*. Why would these sinners be drawn to a man of doom and gloom?

The writers of the gospels focused upon creating a brief account of Jesus' life which would reveal his true identity as the Son of God. Even in the terse statements of the Gospels, one catches a glint of the gleam in Jesus' eye when he drew such word-pictures:

> *It is easier for a camel to go through the eye of a needle than for a rich man to enter the kingdom of God.*
>
> *Take the log out of your own eye before you try take to take a splinter out of another's.*

These are glimpses of a humor and attractiveness which drew people from all walks of life to Jesus' side. Some came to be healed. Some came to find fault and criticize. Others were drawn out of curiosity. But that does not fully explain the attraction of the thousands who sought him out. Matthew noted that he spoke not like the scribes and Pharisees but as one with authority. Obviously, thousands of people came upon more than one occasion to listen to him speak all day! This is what prompted Jesus to feed the 5000 and the 4000 (not counting women and children). Who knows how many times there were smaller or larger groups who came to hear him? After the first multiplying of the food for the crowds, some came just for the free meal and the show. What must not be overlooked, however, is that this man spoke and acted as no other man before or after him.. There was an underlying and unmistakable positive strength about him. It was this joy that is rarely identified which set him apart. Suffering and joy—sacred balance

Jesus balanced Faith and Work: The human tendency carries most of us to extremes, to see things as black or white, good or bad, very appealing or not at all attractive. Often this has more to do with self image than discernment. It requires the presence of God's person, the Holy Spirit himself, at work within us to create the divine balance which is essential for serving God. It is a good thing when any person recognizes that there are indeed certain ultimate values, that there are some truths which are non-negotiable. It is a bad thing when *truths* become excuses to harm others or when *truths* become blinders which do not allow the *truth holder* to see beyond a very limited personal frame of reference.

The Apostle James identified one of these areas of imbalance exhibited by early Christians as he focused on the inevitable conflict of *faith* and *works*. Two thousand years have not diminished the need to address this very common Christian imbalance.

Here is the problem: our tendency as humans is to either ignore problems, difficulties, or injustices or to tackle them head-on. Whether we choose to ignore or vigorously address these concerns, many will choose to rely upon their own strength almost exclusively. Others will choose to seek another person, an organization or a higher power who will assume the problem for them. Few will do otherwise. In all matters pertaining to ultimate truth, Jesus is the best and most reliable guide.

We see the Son of Man seeking his Father's help continually. On numerous occasions Jesus stated his dependence and reliance upon God for everything he did. The Son of God rose early and stayed up late in order to commune with God. Luke recounts, in the 6th chapter of his gospel, that, before the calling of the twelve disciples, Jesus spent the entire night in prayer Therefore, it is entirely appropriate to identify the actions of Christ as an exercise of intensive faith guided by an insatiable desire to listen to God.

Faith alone, however, does not reveal the total character of the Christ. There were no angels who whisked him from one dusty town to next. He had to walk just like everyone else. He became tired and needed sleep. He lost patience and became irritable. He was continually thronged by masses of people seeking healing and food. He had to work his way through all human limitations except one: he did not have to deal with the consequences of his own sin.

Every recorded event of Jesus' life can be categorized as either faith or work in action. A broader perspective of his life illustrates the divine balance he maintained by trusting God and doing what his hands found to do. It is as if faith was his right hand and obedience was his left. It required both of these hands in order to embrace a child, heal a leper, or be nailed to a cross.

Jesus balanced Hope and Reality: There is a very intriguing observation of Jesus made by the Apostle John regarding Jesus' perception of human character and behavior:

> *Now while he was in Jerusalem at the Passover feast, many saw the miraculous signs he was doing and believed in his name. But Jesus did not entrust himself to them, for he knew all men. He did not need man's testimony about man, for he knew what was in a man.* (John 2:26)

We can be grateful to John for this particular insight into the mind of Christ. Jesus had a very clear picture of the nature of the human condition. He was not operating his life under an illusion common to many humanist thinkers identifying mankind as the source of all knowledge, wisdom, and morality. Jesus did not entrust himself to them because he knew that man was not only created in the image of God, he was also fickle, unreliable, and moody. Jesus recognized furthermore that man was capable of creating lies, deception, and evil in multiple forms. If one does not recognize this divine awareness inherent to Jesus understanding, it is easy to relegate *Jesus/Teacher/Messiah* to a long list of well-intentioned but misguided, perhaps naive, persons who try very hard to do good things, but never quite get it when it comes to the nature of man.

The love of Christ becomes even more compelling when paralleled by his awareness of the human capacity for deceiving self and others. When John says that Jesus knew what was in the heart of man, he is also telling us that Jesus knew, in some way, that the cross, or something like it, was waiting. From scripture alone there is no way to know just how much Jesus knew about future events. In Matthew 24, he clearly stated that, unlike his Father, there were things he did not know: in this case, *the end of the age* which he had predicted. Whether it was innate human perception or divine ability, Jesus had a firm grip on the *real world*. He understood fully that he was not to receive any honor for what he did in this world. He recognized that the subjects of his kingdom were not capable of understanding what he did or why he did it. He knew that there was only one possible conclusion to his decision to obey God. That conclusion was played out on a hill beside two thieves.

The weight of this awareness should have created one with a very sour, negative, pessimistic persona who looked at every encounter with great skepticism. What the record reveals is quite the opposite. Here was a man who eagerly encountered persons from every walk of life. He was interested in their thoughts and questions. He enjoyed telling stories and talking to strangers. He loved little children and they loved him. He healed persons of a broad range of human hurt and disease. To our knowledge he never turned away any person for any reason other than self righteous deceit. This is not the sullen brooding man seeking God in a darkened cave. Jesus was invited to dinner parties, welcomed to the homes of tax collectors (who today would be called the leaders of organized crime); he spent time caring for prostitutes, lepers and beggars. And although the scriptures says specifically that Jesus wept, it is my conviction that Jesus did most of this with a smile on his face. This was because he deeply genuinely loved every person he met. He did not command us to do something which he did not do with his whole being. I believe that when you were around him, even if you disagreed with him, you were aware of his care for you. Something inside told you that he was not just sizing you up; he was anxious to see your best.

He combined an inner awareness of reality with an indefinable but unmistakable sense of hope. Here we catch a glimpse of a quality never seen before and never to be seen again: God and man in complete and perfect unity. Hallelujah! What a Savior!

Jesus balanced Male and Female; Love and Expectation; Grace and Judgment: Throughout the Bible, God is presented equally as a God of *grace* and as a God of *judgment*. He is not one or the other; he is not more one than the other. There is great confusion regarding how God's grace and God's judgment relate to one another. The life of Christ is our best example illustrating this balance within the person of God.

Although the words are not entirely interchangeable, *grace* is motivated by love and *judgment* is motivated by expectation. In everyday human relationships we do not often think in terms of grace and judgment, but as families we are very familiar with love and expectations. In the context of family relationships this God-balance becomes more clear.

God created man and woman, male and female. He gave each of them unique characteristics which were essential not only to the survival of the human race but also to the spiritual growth and well being of the child. It can easily vary from couple to couple, but it is most generally observed that the mothering instinct is to nurture, care, embrace, teach and shield from harm. Fathers typically are cast in the role of provider, protector, teacher, mentor, coach and disciplinarian. Perhaps the greatest challenge of our world is recognizing the sanctity and value of these God-given sexual role models for the nurturing and wholeness of children. These models are not rigid guidelines which no man or woman should cross. They are more generally understood as simply the way most men and women are naturally "wired". In healthy couples where this role is altered, it is interesting to note that the same balance is almost always vigorously pursued even if roles are reversed.

Balancing love and expectation is an essential of human growth and most parents do it without even thinking about it. There is a need within every human to receive roughly equal amounts of both unconditional love and loving expectation. Children who receive massive love with no expectations can become monsters of selfish demand. Children who receive massive demands upon their lives, without love, can become calloused authoritarians, compulsive achievers, and, sometimes, abusive bullies.

What we see in the God/Man Jesus Christ is the character reflection of his father. God is both gender and above gender. God chose to be identified as a male parent: *Father*. God chose to send his *son* rather than his daughter. However, there are simultaneously very good reasons to recognize that God is indeed both male and female. Unlike his creations, God is not limited to one sex. Everything about the nature and character of God exhibits both strong male and strong female tendencies. That is why it is important to recognize that being made in God's image applies equally to male and female, recognizing neither as superior but both as essential.

Some may ask then: why Father rather than Mother? The answer to this question lies in the manner which scripture identifies *Father*. The *father ideal* promoted by scripture recognizes the need for authority within the family. This authority is never license to bully or abuse; it is a command to serve unselfishly, to literally lay down his life, if necessary, for his family's welfare. The Bible offers numerous examples of men who abused authority and did great harm to their families. There are also numerous examples of women who undermined their husband's authority and led their families to ruin.

When the father abandons his responsibility to assume authority for his family' welfare, the family is in jeopardy. Even though she may strongly resist the idea, this authority is frequently assumed by the mother for the welfare of family members. Authority can be abused. Lack of authority means ultimate chaos.

The existence of authority within the family in no way diminishes the need for nurturing and love. In every sense, God *mothers* his people. There are numerous examples where God's actions are mothering actions. Jesus was the greatest *authority,* the greatest king who ever walked the earth, yet he never picked up a sword or spear. He never led an army of men into battle. He never held a position or owned a business. Jesus spent his time caring for the sick and lame, healing and restoring individuals to health: physically, mentally, emotionally and spiritually. This was nurturing mother in its greatest moment. God, and the Son in his reflection, displayed and balanced the best of both sexual roles.

Within the Bible, there are numerous examples of really good women and really good men. There are many examples of destructive mothers and destructive fathers.. The role of father which scripture elevates and encourages is the role of provider, protector and lover and teacher. The role of mother which scripture exalts is sacrificial servant, loving caregiver, teacher and encourager.

Perhaps the first question to be addressed is more basic: why does God choose either sex as his chosen manner of identity? Looking back at previous comments, it is quite apparent that God is greater than a single gender. However, because it is not the way of God's choosing, it is misleading and inappropriate to speak of God as asexual, as a thing, or an idea, or an evanescent power. God, creator and sustainer, has chosen to reveal himself most specifically in the role of loving, caring Father who often assumes the role of nurturing mother.

All this discussion is required to grasp a concept of Jesus' balance of grace and judgment, love and expectation. It is very difficult to argue that anyone loved more than Jesus. In obedience to his Father's will, Jesus submitted to the cross willingly in behalf of all mankind. If that isn't love, we have no concept of love's meaning. There is no way to buy or earn the gift of Christ's sacrifice. It is totally free and completely unearned. It is grace, pure and simple. With this grace, however, come some very specific expectations. His words are stern and unbending:

> *Then he said to them all: If anyone would come after me, he must deny himself and take up his cross daily and follow me. For whosoever wants to save his life will lose it, but whosoever loses his life, for me, will save it.* (Luke 9:23-24)

> *Anyone who loves his father or mother more than me is not worthy of me; anyone who loves his son or daughter more than me is not worthy of me.* (Matthew 10:37)

> *No servant can serve two masters. Either he will hate the one and love the other, or he will be devoted to the one and despise the other. You cannot serve both God and Money.* (Luke 16:13)

Then, as now, there were those who wanted grace without expectation. Jesus abruptly dismissed those who wanted a cheap grace:

> *As they were walking along the road, a man said to him, "I will follow you wherever you go." Jesus replied, "Foxes have holes and birds of the air have nests, but the Son of Man has no place to lay his head." He said to another man, "Follow me." But the man replied, "Lord, first let me go and bury my father." Jesus said to him, "Let the dead bury their own dead, but you go and*

proclaim the kingdom of God. Still another said, "I will follow you, Lord; but first let me go back and say good-bye to my family." Jesus replied, "No one who puts his hand to the plow and looks back is fit for service in the kingdom of God. (Luke9:57-62)

In contrast, Jesus corrected James and John (whom he had nicknamed *the sons of thunder'*) because they insisted upon judgment without grace:

When the disciples James and John saw this they asked, "Lord do you want us to call fire down from heaven to destroy them?" But Jesus turned and rebuked them and they went to another village. (Luke 9:54)

The love of God that is channeled through Christ's sacrifice is not dependent upon behavior, appreciation, or obedience. But that love, by its very nature, will not let us go. God's love perseveres through all our objections to take us constantly to new levels of joy which we may not be seeking. His love may be taking us to places we do not know exist. His love *expects* to take us to our finest behavior and then home to share his eternal glory.

It would have been very appropriate if God had chosen to identify himself as *Ultimate Creator* or *Power Beyond All Power*. It would have been equally appropriate to identify himself as the *Source of all Knowledge and Wisdom* but that is not what he chose to do. God chose to identify himself first and foremost as a human parent, as *Father*. It must be remembered that any name for God is inadequate. The Bible uses an exhaustive list of names for God, each identifying only a portion of his greatness. In the midst of all the names appropriate for God, his first choice was *Dad* (Abba father). Supreme deity chose to identify himself as *Dad*, always to be illustrated by the life of his Son. God is to be seen as *Dad,* exactly as we see Jesus who perfectly walks the balance of love and expectation, who balances the roles of male and female, who is lives eternally as righteous judgment and unending grace.

Our Father who art in heaven, Hallowed be thy name!

Jesus balanced past, present, and future:

> *He said to them: Therefore every teacher of the law who has been instructed about the kingdom of heaven is like the owner of a house who brings out of his storeroom new treasures as well as old.* (Matthew 13:52)

John begins his gospel declaring that Jesus existed in the beginning before the world was created. Within his gospel he declares that Jesus was born into the world and lived in it. He concludes his gospel in a conversation in which the resurrected Jesus twice mentions his return. Later writing in exile on the island of Patmos, he records the book of the Apocalypse (Revelation) furthering the image of Christ as ruler of the world that is to come.

It is natural for most persons to gravitate to only one element of time. Most of us know people, usually older, who spend a good portion of their lives focusing on yesterday. Others are fascinated by the future and its intriguing possibilities. Some find their greatest interest in the here and now of current events and daily developments. Books and novels reflect the passion for old and new and now. Science fiction has many authors and many readers. Just a few paces down the library aisle there are large numbers of books glorifying the *Old West*. Not far beyond are thousands of books which are marketed because they seek to promote a new diet plan or stress-reliever or a way to make it big in investing.

Jesus was pressured to choose one time zone and stay in it. The Jewish leaders demanded that Jesus remain in the past tense. He could have been a national sensation and risen to power among the Jews if he had agreed to remain solely within the teaching of Moses and the Talmud.

The followers of Jesus pressured him to confine himself to the future tense, to become the Messiah, the reincarnation of David which they had awaited for centuries.

The Roman government insisted that Jesus must remain in the present, here and now, as a dutiful subject of the Roman empire.

Jesus succeeded in severely disappointing each of them. The Jewish leaders, of course, finally had enough and conspired to have him killed. Since the Jewish authorities did set into motion the death of Christ, it is only speculation, but if they had not, it is very likely that either Rome or Jesus' own followers would have killed him. Jesus' power was too great to ignore. If Jesus is not willing to carry our banner, they would have reasoned, it is best to eliminate him and to do it now.

We as individual believers are most comfortable as we place the living Christ in one exclusive time zone also. Depending upon the believers' individual circumstance, we seek Christ's presence almost exclusively as a past event, a present help, or a future hope. Rarely is he seen as all three.

When Christ is relegated to the past he is enshrined but typically ignored. He is part of the cultural mix of many ethnic and religious cultures. He has a place of recognition, and some honor, but it is long ago and far away. He is a good guy, but he has little to say to the fast pace and demanding world of *today*.

When Christ is relegated to the present day or moment, He can quickly become another tool on the belt of busy technicians, a quick-fix to the complexities of life in which speed is the essence. Help me Jesus, and make it quick! If you do not make it quick, I will go to one of the thousands of other popularly promoted remedies available. It might be yoga, mind control, vegetarianism, or new age thought. When Jesus is only *now,* in a strange twist of divinity, He becomes my servant existing to meet my need.

When Jesus is relegated exclusively to the future, He has all the qualities of a comprehensive insurance policy. There is a premium to be paid for sure, but with that check in the mail, one is free to pursue one's own life without the hindrance of moral restraint, compassion, or community responsibility. With eternal life, religion, and philosophical questions out of the way, one is able to pursue wealth, fame, prestige or power without hindrance.

To declare Jesus as Lord is to declare him as Lord of time. *Kairos* and *chronos* are two Greek words differentiating time. In overly simplified terms, *Chronos* is clock time and *Kairos* is appropriate time. Jesus is Lord of both.

His Kingdom is eternal. His kingdom has a clock. Although these statements seem completely contradictory, the Lordship of Christ overshadows both aspects of time in the exact balance of God's choosing. Christ knows what time it is on the watch you are wearing. He also knows what time it is in eternity and where you are in your time in eternity. He knows when we usually choose to eat supper. He also knows the best time for us to offer help to a neighbor in need. It is only by listening to his Spirit within us that we have any idea of His time. A major element of living the Christian life meaningfully demands the pursuit of God's *chronos* and *kairos* time in all things. It does not take long for the slowest among us to recognize that the best thing at the wrong time can easily become the worst thing, regardless of our intentions.

Jesus balanced the Word of God with the Word of God: One of the greatest strengths of the Bible is its inherent balance. It is not possible to pick a subject relevant to human life that is not addressed by God's word. The word *computer,* the instrument I am now facing, is not recorded in the Bible. The words *airplane*, *technology*, and *Buick* are also missing. However, each of these words and thousands like them represent the thoughts, ideas, ethics, inventions and imaginations of man which are inherent to the pages of God's word. But that is not all.

Every good has an inherent evil. Every evil has an inherent good. It all depends upon the manner and motive in which it is applied. Therefore, in order to present truth, it must always be presented from the insight of balance. It is a good thing to say: Eating carrots is a healthy practice. However, if you eat nothing but carrots, you will die.

It is Christ's way to say:

> *If you are struck on one cheek, turn the other cheek also.* (Matthew 5:39)

It is also Christ's way to say

> *If you harm one of His little ones it would be better for you if you were cast into the sea with a millstone tied to your neck.* (Matthew 18:6)

Christ said,

Love your enemies and do good to those who abuse you. (Matthew 5:44)

He also took up a piece of rope, and on more than one occasion, drove the merchants and money changers from the Jerusalem Temple by sheer brute force (John 2). Jesus refused to tolerate the desecration of his Father's house.

Jesus was confronted by the balance of God's word in almost everything he did. The Pharisees were constantly questioning his actions in light of Rabbinic law based upon Jewish scripture, the Torah (the first five books of the Bible). They questioned him many times:

- when the disciples ate grains of wheat as they walked on the Sabbath day

- when he chose to heal on the Sabbath

- when his disciples did not wash their hands ceremonially (15)

Jesus was constantly accused of violating specific chapter and verse scriptures by the Jewish leaders.

In a great twist of irony, when Satan came to tempt Christ in the wilderness just as he was beginning the time of his public ministry, Satan's temptations were based upon a knowledge of Hebrew scripture! It is very helpful to recognize that the son of God himself was frequently confronted by Satan and by people with very different agendas regarding the interpretation of the Bible. The Bible is the greatest source of truly reliable information regarding the nature and person and revelation of God in existence. However, like any written document, the words can be readily abused and their intended meaning completely corrupted.

So how in the world do we know what to believe? This question opens the door to a larger study of scriptural interpretation which goes far beyond the scope of this writing. However, it is most important for the Christian to understand that the Bible always contains a degree of balance which, properly understood, short circuits the tremendous abuse which is readily possible.

In this regard Satan is a good teacher. It was only with his knowledge of the Messiah promised in Scripture that he was able to pose temptations to Christ. In the second temptation Satan quotes Psalm 91:11-12. In each of the three temptations Jesus responds with a scripture to counter Satan's temptation.

There is almost always a scripture somewhere to back up any evil imaginable. If the scripture is quoted only in part, taken out of context, or connected to other unrelated scriptures it is possible for the Bible to say almost anything. A common example would be combining Matthew 27:5 with Luke 10:37:

> *He (Judas Iscariot) went and hanged himself...Go thou and do likewise.*

We can be very grateful that the word of God maintains a very careful balance in all its pages. Without this balance some very good guidelines quickly become legal rules which are far from the heart of God. When Jesus was accused of violating the Rabbinic Sabbath observances he replied to his accusers:

> *Then he said to them, "The Sabbath was made for man, not man for the Sabbath.* (Mark 2:27)

Two truths stand side by side in this superb teaching:

- God commanded the observance of the Sabbath because it was a protective measure to see that man both rested and took time for God;

- The Sabbath observance was a blessing made for man by God, not a rule to be enforced.

These two statements taken together form a balanced perspective of God's word. Paul was careful to note the importance of this subject:

He has made us competent as ministers of a new covenant --not of the letter but of the Spirit; for the letter kills, but the Spirit gives life. (2 Corinthians 3:6)

Recognizing the balance inherent to the Bible's teaching is in no way to imply that God's word is all conditional, relative or based entirely on subjective thinking. There are many scriptural absolutes. But it must always be understood that the Bible must be understood in the light of itself. Otherwise, seen only as bits and pieces occasionally strung together, the light quickly turns to darkness. As the light of the world, Christ leads us by the power of the Holy Spirit to a balanced understanding of His word.

In conclusion, we see Jesus as an attentive and obedient Son who reflected his Father's image with every breath. His temptations were very real but not always recorded. Jesus' greatest temptation was to allow good things to become more important than God's things. This is also our great temptation. Jesus, like you and I, was tempted to ignore the *Sacred Balance* which is the nature of divinity in itself.

*We can be eternally grateful that
He was faithful to His task.*

8. THE DISCIPLINE OF BALANCING

Balance never just happens.

The *Sacred Balance* is never an achievement: it is always a pursuit. It requires courage and commitment. It requires more than a little stubbornness coupled with more than a little humility and caution.

Balance never happens all alone or in isolation. Balance by its very nature requires harmony of all the individual parts. Balance rarely occurs following a casual interest. Balancing is hard demanding work that threatens our values and our security. Why bother?

Following the example of Jesus, the Christian disciple begins to see the deeply essential necessity of seeking the perspective of a life of *sacred balance*. Finding that balance may be life's most difficult task. Why one would choose to seek the *Sacred balance* originates from positive and negative truths:

- the rewards of pursuing balance are great enough to more than justify the effort

- the consequences of avoiding the pursuit of balance are catastrophic.

The purpose of this chapter is to explore the ways in which the *sacred balance* is indeed achieved and practiced in everyday realities. Make no mistake about it, this is a life-long pursuit which requires significant time, energy and personal honesty. It is not automatic. It is never a completed task. Every day and often every hour demands rebalancing efforts. No other person or program or system can do it for you. Balancing never just happens. It is a demanding intentional effort.

Balance needs to be seen not so much as a quality as a it is a discipline. Richard Foster's book *The Celebration of Discipline* has become a modern classic extolling the values of ancient Christian disciplines (16) In this excellent work, Foster identifies the disciplines of: meditation, prayer, fasting, and study which he calls *inward* disciplines. *Outward* disciplines include simplicity, solitude, submission and service. These are followed by *corporate* disciplines including confession, worship, guidance, and celebration. Foster's primary contention in this writing is that the *disciplines* provide the foundation for meaningful Christian growth and living.

Foster's premise is sound and this book rang a much needed bell within the Christian world. Within the church of North America more time and energy was being expended in pursuit of the values of the corporate business world than in the pursuit of God's values and principles. Far too little time was being spent pursuing God. The Christian life suffers and dies apart from the God-given, God-directed disciplines of Christian discipleship.

What is missing from Foster's book and is indeed the next logical step, is the integration of these disciplines into individual lives, families and organizations. Such is the work of the discipline of balance.

No one would argue that prayer is a bad thing. However, when prayer is not integrated with meditation, fasting, and study it quickly becomes remote and out of touch. At its worst, prayer can become a source of tremendous pride, highly critical and viciously judgmental. This was exactly the situation Jesus described in his parable of the Pharisee and the Tax collector:

> *To some who were confident of their own righteousness and looked down on everybody else, Jesus told this parable: "Two men went up to the temple to pray, one a Pharisee and the other a tax collector. The Pharisee stood up and prayed about himself: 'God, I thank you that I am not like other men—robbers, evildoers, adulterers—or even like this tax collector. I fast twice a week and give a tenth of all I get.' But the tax collector stood at a distance. He would not even look up at heaven, but beat his breast and said, 'God, have mercy on me, a sinner' I tell you that this man, rather than the other, went home justified before God. For everyone who exalts himself will be humbled, and he who humbles himself will be exalted."* (Luke 18: 9-14)

The disciplines of solitude and simplicity can quickly degenerate into a new level of legalism and extreme self-pride when the disciplines of submission and service are absent.

From a corporate perspective, the disciplines of celebration, guidance and worship are not only powerless but destructive when there is no element of confession. This truth applies to every discipline. Out of balance, the strength of the discipline becomes a weakness. A bigger picture emerges. **It has to work together or it does not work at all!**

This awareness causes one to realize that somewhere in the mind of God, He created everything to be alive, to function, grow and prosper only in harmony with the rest of His creation.

What is desperately needed on every level of human existence is the exercise of the integrating discipline, the discipline of balance. The discipline of balance seeks to find and fit in all the pieces to avoid the pitfalls of personal preference in order to truly see the heart of God. The exercise of this discipline requires more work and time than all the rest. Why? The exercise of the discipline of balance demands a deep respect and an intimate awareness of the other disciplines as well as the direction of the Holy Spirit, particularly in the matter of time.

A very good thing at the wrong time is the wrong thing. Most of us as Christians are strongly tempted to take the limited knowledge and/or experiences of our lives and project them on to the screen of our Christian brothers and sisters lives and say: "See, I have found it! Here is truth!, and hope!, and fulfillment!, and holiness! And…" Later, often much later, we see that we had seen only a part of the picture and there was much more yet to be revealed.

Our loving God has great patience with our tendency to globalize our minute experiences until they begin to harm other persons. And then, God becomes our enemy. We often attribute to Satan's power the difficulties we create by promoting the half-truths of unbalanced theology.

Balance as a Corporate Discipline: The discipline of balance has both personal and corporate elements. Much of this writing has focused on the individuals need for balanced living and thinking. The discipline of thinking balance corporately is a field rich with promise.

Paul writing to the Church of Ephesus has been problematic to the church as he outlines five distinct shapes of ministry to the church. It is not clear whether these are offices to be held by individuals within the church or spiritual gifts given by the Holy Spirit for the purpose of leadership. Some contend they are only personal talents evidenced within some individuals more than others.

> *It was he who gave some to be apostles, some to be prophets, some to be evangelists, and some to be pastors and teachers, to prepare God's people for works of service, so that the body of Christ may be built up until we all reach unity in the faith and in the knowledge of the Son of God and become mature, attaining to the whole measure of the fullness of Christ.* (Ephesians 4:11-13)

Christian denominations approach this scripture differently. Some choose to ignore it entirely. Evangelicals have tended to lump all of these functions into one role usually identified as *pastor*. Mainline churches do the same with different titles: Priest, Rector, Deacon, etc.

Ephesians 4 in its entirety can be identified as a balancing document intended for churches of all time. The specific naming of apostle, prophet, evangelist, pastor and teacher recognizes the necessity of employing varying abilities to work in harmony in the life of the church. Paul the Apostle recognized the need for the discipline of balance in the life and operation of the church

This scripture reminds its readers of two primary truths. First, no one individually can do it all; and, second, groups which do not have persons with differing specific capabilities are inadequate for the task to build up the body of Christ.

The discipline of balance is extremely challenging on a personal level. On a corporate level it is even more challenging, but no less essential. Steven Covey's best selling book *The Seven Habits of Highly Effective People*, devotes three of the seven habits to corporate issues. (17) One of the great values of this work is Covey's insistence on the necessity of seeking solutions which involve people on all levels. What emerges is the need for the discipline of balance which goes beyond individual concerns and sees the organization as a living organism. Covey's insights apply to any organization of any size. His great wisdom lies in his awareness that every person within the group has a crucial role to fulfill. You cannot leave out the janitor when you are looking at the health of the organization! When individuals are overlooked or devalued it effects every aspect of the organization.

This truth could also be stated in balance terms by saying that

without the balanced functioning of the whole machine, it ain't gonna work!

The Discipline of Balance and the Holy Spirit: Before we pack up our tools and go to work on the discipline of balance it is extremely important to recognize the working of the Holy Spirit, the third person of the Trinity, in this very difficult process. Jesus identifies this person as *the Spirit of truth*, and one of his functions is to guide believers into all truth.

> *But when he, the Spirit of truth, comes, he will guide you into all truth. He will not speak on his own; he will speak only what he hears, and he will tell you what is yet to come.* (John 16:13)

THE DISCIPLINE OF BALANCING

A significant portion of the discipline of balance requires reliable information and good human reasoning. (Three pieces of chocolate cake is probably too much). However, a healthy portion of the discipline of balance requires insight and understanding that goes beyond human reason alone. The biblical record reveals a number of occasions when God directed his servants to do things which outwardly had nothing to do with reason and had balance only because God commanded it!

It would be difficult to see any balance in God's command to Isaiah to go naked for thee years(!) as a sign of God's judgment against Egypt and Cush.(18) It is doubtful that Jeremiah saw a lot of balance when he was pulled out of a vaulted cell in a dungeon only to be lowered into a cistern of mud in the courtyard of the guard:

> *King Zedekiah then gave orders for Jeremiah to be placed in the courtyard of the guard . . . So they (the officials of the city) took Jeremiah and put him into the cistern of Malkijah, the king's son, which was in the courtyard of the guard. They lowered Jeremiah by ropes into the cistern; it had no water in it, only mud, and Jeremiah sank down into the mud.* (Jeremiah 37:21 and 38:6)

When his brothers sold him as a slave, balance was not uppermost in Joseph's mind. The scales of balance are held by the hand of God.

In addition to study (reason), those who seek the discipline of balance must first enter through the doors of prayer, meditation, fasting and, almost always, waiting. The discipline of balance requires the simultaneous application of both faith and reason. In most instances, either faith or reason assumes greater power. It is almost sacrilege to speak of *reason* on the same plane with *faith*. Faith is the uppermost guiding principle of the Christian life. That faith, however, must be applied appropriately to the time and circumstance of its occurrence. The Holy Spirit is equally at work in both areas and the discipline of balance seeks His help in bringing them together. Trying to balance anything without the direct assistance and guidance of the Holy Spirit is futile and potentially very damaging.

The Big Picture

The discipline of balance is a critical need in in every area of life, but as a discipline, balance is almost completely ignored. There are no courses in universities or seminaries or business colleges dealing with balance. It is taken for granted that balance will occur. It is assumed that leadership and management will see things the same way at the same time. It is assumed that church leadership and church membership will see plans and programs as equally important. It is assumed that planning programs and activities will not require leaders and members as well as careful listening, consultation, and regular periods of review. It is assumed that the architects and engineers, the framers, carpenters and plumbers and electricians will all see the building in just the same way.

There are no courses in *Beginning Balance*. One cannot acquire a graduate degree in *Balance*. Imagine a doctoral thesis on *Integrating the use of military weapons in the pursuit of World Peace*. Whether we like it or not, this is the world we occupy. It is well and good to seek the ideals of peace and brotherly concern. These ideals cannot ignore parents who are paid for the employment of children as suicide bombers.

Nobody wants what everybody needs.

There is no person, no family, no organization small or large, no church, no denomination, no town or village or city, no state or province or country, no political party or non-profit organization which can exist without a dedicated periodic review of essential priorities. Balance or decline are the only options.

Balance is not a panacea to all of life's problems. Balance will not cure cancer or make people love those they hate. Balance will not solve all the problems. Balance can, however, keep us on the road.

Exercising the discipline of balance will force one to see things from something other than the narrow perspective of individual prejudice. It will make us aware that there are different ways to look at the problems which have seemed impossible. The discipline of balance will enable us to see some others in a totally new light of deepening appreciation. Balance is the ability to stay on the road. It will also keep us on the highway while others are in the ditch and out of control.

If we are getting the idea that the discipline of balance is extremely demanding- we are on the right road. The discipline of balance refuses the temptation to pick favorites. Every piece of the puzzle is indispensable to the creation of the whole picture.

9. HIGH ROAD LONELY ROAD

If the reader has had the patience to read this far, it is likely that he/she is beginning to think about some issues of balance in their own personal lives. If that is indeed the case, this book has been worth the effort. It is necessary to bring a certain reality to the table of this discussion. The subtitle of this book, *Nobody wants what everyone needs*, is a necessary reminder.

As humans we do not like or enjoy thinking about balance. What we do without thinking at all in the process of walking comes only at great effort in the process of our thinking. We do not think balance. We think preferences. I greatly prefer sunshine rather than rain. I think sunshine, and I have to adjust to rain, even though I know that rain is absolutely necessary to everything that lives. I greatly prefer fall to winter. I think fall. I have to adjust to winter. I greatly prefer following my own schedule rather than the dictates of conferences or work schedules. I think freedom. I have to adjust to schedules. So it is with each of us. Every person has likes and preferences which are usually normal and good and are simply expressions of one's unique personality.

The problem arises in those things we do not especially care for to which we must adjust. Most people are able to see the need for balance but because it means change or causes us to do things which are not pleasant, we resist the balance which is essential to our health, our business, our family, our life.

Nobody wants what everybody needs.

The truly exceptional people of our world are not those who choose just one course and never deviate from it. Sadly, these persons are most often seen as heroes or successes worthy of emulation. The true heroes in every aspect of life are those brave men and women who refuse to see life with the tunnel vision so often necessary to achieve success by most standards. The truly great men and women are those who see the picture from a perspective larger than most and recognize that there must be balance before there is genuine success.

The career of my wife Jeanne serves to illustrate this very well. Jeanne is the quintessential kindergarten teacher. This year she completes forty years of shaping and loving and guiding little people into the world of education, socialization, group dynamics, personal hygiene, family values and self worth.

She strongly adheres to Robert Fulghum's book: *Everything I Need to Know I Learned In Kindergarten*. She has had over 1200 children under her immediate care in the last forty years. That would not account for the 2000+ parents of these children or the unknown number of siblings who were also taught or affected by *Mrs. Blackmon's* care.

Mrs. Blackmon has never experienced a year in her professional life when balance has not been a major struggle within her world. Even in kindergarten there are constant ongoing struggles for power.

"Hands are made for helping, not hurting" is never a settled issue as eager young students move out of the confines of home into the larger world. This has to be balanced with the recognition that every child desperately needs to be touched and loved by this person in authority.

Within her classroom there are often students of varying backgrounds. *Mrs. Blackmon* adamantly insists that she does not teach Caucasian children, Chinese children, Native children, or Slavic children: she teaches little people who are uniquely individual with distinctive needs and concerns. She does not teach *minorities*. She teaches **children** and loves them in every color and every manner of dress and from every background.

Parents are a particular challenge and joy to the kindergarten teacher. Every parent of every child is extremely sensitive to the welfare of their *baby*. Parents come in all degrees of health and sickness. It is very tempting to adjust rules or procedures in order to keep difficult or overly demanding parents happy, just to keep them off your back. But that happens only at the expense of little lives.

Therefore, *Mrs. Blackmon* has to wade regularly into civil battle with parents who are often young and new at parenting. She works very hard to be kind and courteous and thoughtful of their concerns, but she will not back down from issues that she believes to be critical to the care of the student/child and the welfare of the group. Many are the disgruntled, offended young parents who have come later to see her wisdom and thanked her for helping them to see what they could not.

Administration plays a powerful role in the life of every teacher. Administration can be very helpful and supportive. Administration can also become agenda-driven and highly insensitive to the needs of the children. Usually it is a little of both. It is very common for administrators who started out as teachers to become so removed from the classroom that they forget the importance of the trials and struggles which exist there. Concerns over finance, enrollment numbers, school board issues and raw personal ambition often color administrative policy far more than seeking solutions which are appropriate for the children, teachers and schools involved. When that occurs, and it occurs regularly, *Mrs. Blackmon* seeks in the most professional manner possible to convey to the powers that be that they have deviated from the primary purpose for which the school exists: the education and growth of children.

By bringing all these factors together, a telling picture emerges. The constantly recurring picture in the life of the kindergarten teacher I have lived with for forty years is something like this: Mrs. Blackmon, driven by an undivided love for children, finds herself

- frequently at odds with the harmful behavioral problems within some children which threaten the welfare of others;

- frequently at odds with parents who neglect their children or have harmful goals for them:

- frequently at odds with administration when programs precede the needs of children as priorities

- sometimes at odds with her husband because she works too hard.

This is a true real-life picture of balance at work. It is not an easy task. It involves tears and long, long hours and periods of excruciating self-doubt. But, the record will show that there are over 1200 children and many parents and teaches and administrators who have greatly benefited because of one person's insistence on the high road lonely road of balanced living.

If You Go—

If you have the stamina to pursue balance, do not expect the world to rise up and call you blessed. Do not expect to be the one who is picked by the boss for the next advancement. Do not expect your colleagues to admire or support you. Some will, and you really want to hold on to them, because they are true and real.

Some mention has been made earlier of the loneliness that often accompanies the pursuit of the *Sacred Balance*. Most of us occasionally enjoy our little pity trips, convinced that the world is out to get us. Hopefully these are short journeys that quickly return to the sunshine. Yet, the traveler must recognize that the great numbers of people in any group are always on the right, or on the left, and there are very few in the middle of the road. Walking the *Sacred Balance* often demands traversing a lonely road.

It is very doubtful that one can become or remain a politician and truly seek balance. Politicians who seek balance succeed best in making both sides angry. The ones who do succeed in addressing and creating balance are very rare and very precious to any nation's history. They have transcended politics. They have become statesmen.

In order to make him look more attractive to some, Jesus Christ has been depicted as a radical, a revolutionary, as one who threw out all the old for something new and great. Although there are elements of truth in this thought, this is not the best picture of the Christ.

The Messiah and Savior described by scripture is the picture of a very attentive and very obedient Son who did nothing which His Father did not command him to do. In doing what his Father commanded, the Christ refused to compromise the picture of God he was called to create. Jesus died at the cross because God's love was bigger than anything mankind had to put it in. Man's love is always weighted by preference. God's love is balanced and available to all.

You can call it love, you can call it balance. Either way it has great cost and tremendous healing effect. It is my prayer that as you pursue a life of balance you will experience the power of the living Christ and the joy of walking with Him...

...right down the middle of the road.

ENDNOTES

Chapter Two

(1) Christian, C. Wallace. "The Man in the Middle," *The Baylor Line*. Waco, Texas: September, 1991.

Chapter Four

(2) Blackmon, Bill D. Faithful For The Season (Saskatoon: Little Print Shop on 8th), 2001.
(3) Peck, M. Scott. The Road Less Traveled. (New York: Bantam Books, 1986).
www.statueofresponsibility.com

Chapter Five

(4) Packer, J. I. Knowing God. (Downer's Grove: Intervarsity Press) ,1979.

Chapter Six

(5) Covey, Steven. Principle-Centered Leadership. (New York: Simon and Schuster), 1990.

Chapter Seven

(6) Bonocore, Mark. "Jesus' Brothers and Mary's Perpetual Virginity." (Evangelical Catholic Apologetics website)
(7) Mark 3:21, Mark 6:4, John 7:3-5
(8) 1 Corinthians 15:7

(9) 2 Kings 2:23-24
(10) Matthew 19 and Matthew 21
(11) Trueblood, D. Elton. Humour of Christ. (San Francisco: Harper Books), 1975.
(12) Luke 8: 1-3
(13) John 20, 26, 29; John 21:15; Acts 1:3
(14) John 19:23-24; Luke 8:1-3; Matthew 17:27 and 37
(15) Matthew 12-15

Chapter Eight

(16) Foster, Richard J. Celebration of Discipline, (San Francisco: Harper), 1978.
(17) Covey, Steven. Seven Habits of Highly Effective People (New York: Simon and Schuster), 1989.
(18) Isaiah 20:3

Printed in the United States
69691LV00002B/4-99